THE MINISTRY AND MYTH

of

THE FIRST LADY

CLIFFORD E. TURNER, PhD

CREATION HOUSE

A STRANG COMPANY

THE MINISTRY AND MYTH OF THE FIRST LADY
by Clifford E. Turner, PhD
Published by Creation House
A Strang Company
600 Rinehart Road
Lake Mary, Florida 32746
www.creationhouse.com

This book or parts thereof may not be reproduced in any form, stored in a retrieval system, or transmitted in any form by any means—electronic, mechanical, photocopy, recording, or otherwise—without prior written permission of the publisher, except as provided by United States of America copyright law.

Unless otherwise noted, all Scripture quotations are from the King James Version of the Bible.

All scripture definitions are taken from *Strong's Exhaustive Concordance* unless otherwise noted.

Cover design by Rachel Campbell

Copyright © 2007 by Clifford E. Turner
All rights reserved

Library of Congress Control Number: 2007924909
International Standard Book Number: 978-1-59979-185-2

First Edition

07 08 09 10 11 — 9 8 7 6 5 4 3 2 1
Printed in the United States of America

CONTENTS

The First Lady has been such a vital, yet obscure, function in the church, often generating much debate regarding the validity of her role. Many church leaders neglect the position of First Lady, considering it unbiblical and nonessential. Others overemphasize and abuse the function and authority of the pastor's wife and help to breed the stereotype of the big-hat-wearing, non-stop-shopping, big-jewelry-wearing, looking-good, but-having-no-real-substance woman behind the man of God.

This book, without debating the validity or biblical correctness of the role, addresses the characteristics that are necessary for every First Lady, pastor, or other woman of God in ministry. All too often, we in the kingdom of God, have failed to be trained. We have failed to receive wisdom regarding our various roles, responsibilities, and expectations (both God's and men's). The Bible says, "My people are destroyed for lack of knowledge" (Hosea 4:6)—not for lack of prayer, lack of conferences, lack of fasting, or lack of prophetic words—*lack of knowledge!* The Bible further states, "And with all thy getting get understanding" (Prov. 4:7) In a society that now often lacks many of the foundational essentials that were taught in the home, there is an unprecedented need to address issues that at one time may have been thought to be "common."

My husband, Dr. Clifford E. Turner, has written this book in his never-ending quest to help women in ministry who have been placed in areas of great authority and responsibility. This book was written from the notes of a First Lady's class, taught by my husband for women who believed that God was calling them into ministry. I was a student of the class (taught over twelve years ago), although not his wife at the time (that's another book!). I can attest to the honesty, validity, and need for many of these issues to be addressed. Even for those of us who know many of the requirements, *The Ministry and Myth of the First Lady,* helps us to reexamine ourselves, to "see if we be in the faith," and to have our "call" confirmed.

In many of the references in this book, my husband refers to his first wife, and my former First Lady, Co-Pastor Denise M. Turner, to whom he was married for over twenty years before she went home to be with the Lord. This book is dedicated to her memory, because she truly exhibited the love, maturity, generosity, wisdom, patience, attitude, sense of family, and commitment to her call of being "The First Lady." She was key in the building of Liberty Temple Full Gospel Church (which began with two members). Since its inception, it has expanded to over fifteen locations nationwide (as of this printing), sixteen nations outside the United States, and a network of thousands of individuals, businesses, and ministries.

My prayer is that every First Lady, woman in ministry, or woman of God seeking to be blameless before our Father, will read this book. The insight and wisdom it contains, when read with an open heart, will help every woman that reads it to ascend to a higher level in faith, love, and character. I trust that you, too, will allow *The Ministry (& Myths) of the First Lady* to aid you in your march towards perfection.

—Elect Lady Darlyn C. Turner

*G*OD HAS ENTRUSTED women with power, influence, and mighty purpose. Personally, a female apostle mentored me, and I have several women pastors in my fellowship. I thank God that they have been godly examples of strength, grace, and humility. However, over the course of my thirty years in ministry, there has seemingly been an uprising of independent and unsubmitted women in ministry that are leading masses of women down the path of pride and arrogance, under the disguise of "freedom."

Please do not get me wrong. There are many wonderful, anointed, submitted, and powerful women of God. However, there are an alarmingly increasing number of women successful in ministry that have gained popularity and prestige, but who are poor examples of loving, caring, and committed virtuous women. God is still calling for the Naomi's of this age to mentor the Ruth's. The wisdom principles of life are still the same as they were over 2000 years ago. A soft answer still turns away wrath and it is still unwise to answer a fool lest you become like him (Prov. 26:4).

Every First Lady, pastor, and Christian must understand that wisdom is the principle component of being successful in life, successful in God, and successful in ministry. The Bible says wisdom is the *principle* thing. This means that wisdom is that which is first in priority, preeminent, and most necessary. Without wisdom, ladies, you, your ministry,

1

your marriage, and your family will die a sure and sudden death. I am not speaking negatively, but the Bible makes it clear that without wisdom, destruction, death, poverty, and shame are inevitable.

First Ladies must be women of wisdom. They must be women who not only seek knowledge, but also learn how to apply it. Otherwise, they will be "ever learning," but never coming into the knowledge of the truth. To put it another way, you can be gifted, know scriptures, prophesy, have revelation, and know how to preach, but if you do not know how to walk in love and patience when it is required in everyday situations, you only have knowledge—and not wisdom.

Women in ministry must be examples of wisdom as wives and mothers, in business and in ministry. Their wisdom and discretion will preserve them and bring them to a place of honor, glory, prosperity, and purpose. Too many First Ladies that I have seen are smart, but not *wise*. A smart woman knows how to save her money, but a wise woman knows how to sow. A smart woman looks out for herself, but a wise woman prefers others over herself. A smart woman stands up for her rights, but a wise woman knows righteousness must transcend rights.

I believe you are a wise woman seeking wisdom, knowledge, correction, and truth—because you are reading this book. I am in agreement with you that you will come into the fullness of Christ and you will walk out the good and perfect will that God has for you, your family, and your ministry.

CHAPTER 1

WHY SATAN IS AFRAID OF WOMEN

And I will put enmity between thee and the woman...

—Genesis 3:15

 $\mathscr{A}$ s A FIRST Lady, woman in ministry, or woman of God, your first order of business is to know that Satan hates you. Therefore, you do not *ever* want to give him a "place" to work in your life. It was established from the beginning that the woman and her seed were the archrivals of Satan himself as Genesis 3:14–15 records:

> And the LORD God said unto the serpent, Because thou hast done this, thou art cursed above all cattle, and above every beast of the field; upon thy belly shalt thou go, and dust shalt thou eat all the days of thy life: And I will put enmity between thee and the woman, and between thy seed and her seed; it shall bruise thy head, and thou shalt bruise his heel.

The word "enmity" is *eybah* in the Hebrew language. It means to have hostility or a deep-seated hatred against. Thus, Satan and the woman have been long-time rivals. God purposely planned for the relationship between the woman and the devil to be this way. Verse 15 initiated the official fight between Satan and mankind.

Satan has a strategy to destroy man, but God has a master plan; and the key to victory in God's plan is the seed of the woman. Every idea, invention, agenda, and purpose on earth comes through a man (referring to mankind) and all of mankind comes through a woman. So, Satan recognizes that when he attacks the woman, it is not just a personal attack, he is attacking "the seed": the ideas, the purpose, and the destiny of whatever she is attempting to birth.

GOD HAS PLACED A SPIRITUAL ALARM INSIDE THE WOMAN.

You need to fully understand that Satan has launched a major demonic assignment against women, not only to stop the seed but also to shut down the call of God on their lives.

Satan hates women because of what God has put inside of them. One thing that God has placed inside the woman is a spiritual alarm. This alarm is very sensitive to the seed or the fruit of the satanic realm because of the fight that has been going on from the beginning of time. Ladies, this is why you are often the only one who can discern trouble and fervently sense Satan's setups. This alarm senses when the family is in trouble; it senses wrong associations; and it senses when things are moving away from the will of God. This alarm is triggered by a natural enmity between the woman and Satan, and it demands confrontation.

We know that God told the woman, in Genesis 3:16, "Thy desire shall be to thy husband, and he shall rule over thee." The word "rule" here is the Hebrew word *mashal*, which means to keep order or to be the head. God's motive for establishing rule was to designate spiritual authority and order in His house, according to His eternal purpose.

The Book of Jeremiah gives us another glimpse into the fullness of the role of the woman and her relationship with the man. Jeremiah 31:22 says:

> How long wilt thou go about, O thou backsliding daughter? for the LORD hath created a new thing in the earth. A woman shall compass a man.

In order to see what God is saying here through the prophet, we will continue to look at key words in the scripture. The word "compass" is the Hebrew word *cabab*, and it means to stand around. When Jeremiah stated that a woman shall compass a man, he was not saying that a woman will rule over him, because God has already established the man as the head. However, he is saying that the woman will compass, surround, or be about the man on every side. In essence, this simply means that in every way and in every place, God will be using a woman as a "watchman" for the man. The woman, therefore, is God's secret intelligence weapon!

The American Amplified Version describes this role of

the woman even further. The word "compass" includes the following in its translation:

- Woo—to achieve, to evangelize
- Win—to reach and to gain loyalty
- Protect—to guard and keep from being attacked, damaged, or stolen

A woman, then, has the anointing and grace to woo, win over, gain loyalty, guard, and protect even a mean, insensitive, or proud man. A woman who knows her power can and will gain the loyalty and respect she deserves. Like the woman with the issue of blood, or the Syrophenecian woman whose daughter was sick, or the woman refusing to leave the judge alone; you can obtain a favorable decision through the grace with which God has already equipped you.

Proverbs 12:4 lets us know that "a virtuous woman is a crown to her husband." "Virtuous" is translated from *chayil* in Hebrew, which means "an army that is war worthy." In other words, to be a virtuous woman, you can't be a punk! This scripture refers to a woman of valor who is bold to do battle.

The word "crown" in this verse literally stands for: "A radar to detect darkness, to encircle or protect, and to compass." So, putting it all together, a war-worthy woman of valor encircles, protects, and detects darkness for her husband. Does this sound like a woman who sits around looking good with no voice and no authority? I can tell you by the Spirit of God that men who have not allowed the women in their lives to give their input, sound the alarm, or operate in their God-given giftings have already allowed the devil to surround, infiltrate, and invade their marriages, their ministries, and their families.

Therefore, men, I admonish you to allow and release the women to surround you in warfare as God has called them to do. You are the head, O king, but your wife is the crown that is called to cover the king's head.

CHAPTER 2

THE FIRST LADY DEFINED

Even so must their wives be grave, not slanderers,
sober, faithful in all things.

—1 Timothy 3:11

$\mathscr{I}$N 1 TIMOTHY 3, the apostle Paul set forth the requirements of the church leaders, particularly the men, admonishing them to be: blameless…sober…of good behavior…apt to teach…not double-tongued…not greedy of filthy lucre, etc. In this chapter, as well as in other books and chapters of the Bible, the requirements for female leaders and First Ladies are also described. (For example, see 1 Timothy 3 and 1 Peter 3.)

However, the core premise of being a First Lady is very simple and can be summed up as this: First Ladies should be "first" in being a "lady."

I believe that the "art" of being a lady has been somewhat lost in today's society. In the quest for freedom, equality, and equal rights, even the church has begun to divert from some of the "old landmarks" that should not be removed. The very term "First Lady" clearly defines the essence of what the individual that holds its title should reflect.

Let's look further into the makeup of the term "First Lady," beginning with the definition of "first."

"First" is defined as:

- Coming before or above all others in time, order, rank or importance.

- Occurring or acting before all others in time; earliest

- Ranking above all others in importance or quality; foremost

"Lady" is defined as:

- A well-mannered and considerate woman with high standards of proper behavior

- A woman regarded as proper and virtuous

- A woman who is the head of a household

- A woman, especially when spoken of or to in a polite way

- A woman of refinement

So, then, what is a First Lady?

"First Lady" is defined as:

A woman who is the head of a household, considered to be foremost in her profession, whose character and behavior ranks above others, and whose positive actions precede others.

"First Lady" has nothing to do with lifting yourself up in pride or haughtiness; or being a big "I" surrounded by little "you's"; but it has everything to do with being first in honor, courage, and responsibility, and being a godly example.

CHAPTER 3

THE CALL

For many are called, but few are chosen.
—Matthew 22:14

HE OFFICE OF a First Lady is just that—an office. It is a place of authority, a position, and a call. The call refers to being invited and summoned. Every woman that stands beside her husband in ministry, whether she can sing or not, play the piano or not, prophesy or not, has been invited and summoned by God to a position of authority and responsibility that requires wisdom, sacrifice, commitment, and understanding.

FIRST LADIES MUST NOT ONLY RECEIVE MENTORING, BUT KNOW ALSO THAT THERE IS A NEED FOR TRAINING.

ACCEPT AND UNDERSTAND THE CALL

You must first consciously and deliberately accept and understand that you have been called. If you do not recognize the call, you are certainly not fulfilling the commission. You must "count up the costs" of this call and make a decision to give up your own life so that the life Christ has for you may be revealed.

There are many women in ministry who have accepted the call to serve God—so they think. However, many have never really accepted the fullness of the call. How do you know? You know because the call to any place in ministry is accepting the call to die! If you refuse to die to your old mind-set, personal preferences, likes, dislikes, doing things your own way, responding negatively to people, and a questionable belief system, you really have not accepted the call.

Every disciple that Jesus called had to walk away from something. Every one of them had to leave that which was familiar—family, traditions, and places—to wholly and completely dedicate themselves to the call.

Some women in ministry pride themselves by saying, "Well, this is just the way I am." What they are really saying is, "I have not developed social skills or the ability to interact with others." To those women God would say, "You have not died yet."

Then, some women have a certain style of dress that is not appropriate for women in ministry; while others fear the loss of their freedom if they come to a certain place of submission. All of these women do not recognize that the price of their call requires a denial of some of their personal preferences, which is, once again, the need to die to self.

Too many saints have just opted to "follow Christ," but failed to "take up their cross." Jesus said, "If any man will come after me, let him deny himself, *and* take up his cross, and follow me" (Matt. 16:24). In other words, you cannot just tiptoe through the tulips, honey. The cross represents suffering, denial, and the dying of your flesh. Unless you first accept the call to die to yourself, you really cannot truly follow Christ.

A favorite hymn that we sang in the Baptist church puts it like this: "Must Jesus bear the cross alone and all the world go free? No, there's a cross for everyone and there's a cross for me."*

Remember, the call to something is always a call *from* something!

ACCEPT THE CALL, COUNT THE
COSTS, AND RESIGN YOURSELF
TO THE DEATH OF SELF.

COUNT UP THE COSTS

Secondly, after you have accepted the call, count up the costs and resign yourself to the death of self (the death of your ways, your ideals, and your thoughts—replacing them

---

* Thomas Shepherd and George N. Allen, "Must Jesus Bear the Cross Alone?"

with God's ways, God's ideals, and God's thoughts). You need to get some understanding and wisdom in how to fulfill this tremendous call so that you may be not only the called, but also the chosen.

I have been in ministry for almost thirty years and I sadly report that too many First Ladies and women in ministry have pursued things: getting speaking engagements, getting jewelry, St. John suits, houses, and land. Sadly, they have forgotten in all of their getting, to get understanding!

~

IT IS THROUGH YOUR RELATIONSHIP WITH GOD THAT YOUR PURPOSE AND CALL WILL TRULY BE REVEALED.

As a First Lady or woman in ministry, you must understand that the most important thing to be is a woman of prayer. Only then, can you operate in power and fulfill God's purpose for your call. It is also important for you to know that your purpose and plan may be drastically different from that of your counterparts. However, it is through your relationship with God, through prayer, and through your submission to the God-ordained authorities in your life that your purpose and call will truly be revealed.

There are key components of your call to ministry that must be understood. Esther is the best example of a First Lady. She was a woman of prayer who submitted herself to the spiritual authority in her life (Mordecai), and she was called for a specific purpose. Therefore, she was able to appropriate God's grace and power. In a nutshell, this is exactly how the kingdom works, whether male or female, First Lady, prophet, or apostle. God has placed a call on your life before the foundations of the world. Then, He puts you in the right family (it was the right one, whether you believe it or not), and assigns you to a spiritual authority figure. As you (like Esther) grow in grace, character, and obedience to both God *and* man, you will be led to your ultimate purpose.

Esther (like most of you) did not ask for this call; she was summoned. Esther was then groomed and prepared for her call. This is a very critical point that has generally been missed in the kingdom of God. Her appointment as queen was just the beginning of her responsibilities and ultimate purpose for her position. She was not placed in the coveted position of queen for her own enjoyment and comfort.

Ladies, I have to stop right here for a moment. I need to be your spiritual Mordecai today and bring some things to your remembrance:

You must stay focused on why you are where God called you. You are not "in the palace" so you can look good, drive good, and live large. Therefore, your daily activities and focus cannot be on fleshly things. You are in the palace to save a nation! You are in the position you are in to reach souls! People will die if you do not fulfill your call!

There are four basic but important principles of the call of being a First Lady that I would like to discuss with you:

PRINCIPLES OF THE CALL:
#1—IT IS NOT ABOUT YOU!

Study the life of Esther and see her attitude when accepting the call. The Bible says that she had favor with all of the people because she was not demanding nor making all kinds of requests. She took the route of humility and, therefore, was exalted by God. The position of First Lady is a spiritual position in the body of Christ, and you must always remember that you were chosen for God's purpose and not your own personal fulfillment. Like Esther, even in times of what may look like your promotion over your mentor, you must yield, relent, and submit to your spiritual authority.

PRINCIPLES OF THE CALL:
#2—YOU MUST STAY HUMBLE.

What would have happened if Esther tried to go in front of the king without prayer, without preparation, without favor, and in her own strength? People who do not pray have an independent spirit. Humility is birthed through prayer and consecration. Esther had favor because of her lifestyle of prayer and her lifestyle of humility. Her three-day consecration just activated the power that was already in her.

PRINCIPLES OF THE CALL:
#3—THE CALL REQUIRES A CONSECRATED LIFESTYLE.

A consecrated lifestyle—a separated and set apart way of living—is necessary to walk in the power that God has for you. Priests, prophets, and all the great men and women of God were called to be separate, even when they were among the people. As a woman in ministry, God requires you to set some relationships apart, some preferences apart, and some time apart to dedicate to His kingdom and for His glory.

I must again emphasize that Esther was a praying woman, which any call in ministry requires one to be. You will not be effective if you do not pray. Please recognize the damage that will be done if you have a call to save or speak to a nation, but you fail to appropriate the power that comes through prayer to fulfill that call.

PRINCIPLES OF THE CALL:
#4—THE CALL, WHEN FULLY OBEYED, BRINGS AUTHORITY, POWER, AND INFLUENCE.

Esther's combination of wisdom and prayer produced a power and influence that set the decree of the Lord. When you, woman of God, operate in wisdom and power in your assigned place, you too will have a level of influence and power unprecedented.

Esther had so much favor that she broke the law and lived! Esther had so much favor that the king offered her half of his kingdom when she broke the law. Esther had so much favor she set the decree without being king! You see, ladies, every woman of God has the power of influence. If you fully obey, you will be able to set precedents, make decrees, and establish order—all from your own bosom. So, don't get caught up in your title; your title will not give you real power with God, but your submission, obedience, wisdom, and humility will.

When you follow all of the principles of the call, it will automatically lead you to a place of power, authority, and influence. The Bible states that, "If ye be willing and obedient, ye shall eat the good of the land" (Isa. 1:19). So, there are benefits and blessings that come along with obedience and the attitude of our hearts as we obey our call.

Remember, the servant-leaders will always be the greatest in the sight of God. Decide today that you are more interested in pleasing God than gaining the popularity and admiration of man. Having the mind of Christ, as we serve others, will always lead to a place of exaltation and honor, but first be humble, because "before honour is humility" (Prov. 15:33). Anyone who has received honor before humility did not receive their honor from God.

REMINDER

Satan needs your fears and insecurities to keep you from being what God purposed for you to be, and keep you locked into your past. Your past is not your potential.

CHAPTER 4

ATTITUDE

A good name is rather to be chosen than great riches, and loving favour rather than silver and gold.

—Proverbs 22:1

HE BIBLE SAYS, "Examine yourselves, whether ye be in the faith" (2 Cor. 13:5). You may have the religious pedigree to be a First Lady and come from a line of ministers. Your mother may have even groomed you to be a First Lady. You may have the "First-Lady-look" down pat—the look of elegance and charm—but do you have the servant's character to walk out this gifted position without being a reproach to the kingdom of God? Your attitude will answer this question. However, I have never known God to give great favor and victory to a person who did not sincerely serve and love.

There must be maturity in
the First Lady that helps
her to move on while
dealing with issues.

Attitude and temperament can be synonymous. All of us have weaknesses in our temperaments and in our personalities. However, ministry is no place for a novice. The devil will make mincemeat out of a "rookie" in ministry, because that person has not yet been tried in ministry's fires. There must be maturity in the First Lady that helps her to move on while dealing with issues. The First Lady must be able to maintain stability in her emotions and in her demeanor while going through various negative situations, like financial problems, marital crises, and all of the other pressures of life.

Some people do not have the maturity to have an argument at home, then, step a foot outside of the house and put on another face. They say, "Well, I just can't be phony." No, this is not being phony; this is being mature. Particularly, as the First Lady, there is a precedent that is set for other women, which is established by the "set woman" out front. King Ahasuerus and his court understood this principle, which is why Vashti, when she refused to obey the request of her king and husband, was abolished from her place of power. Esther 1:15-18 shows the responsibility and accountability of women in such a position.

What shall we do unto the queen Vashti according to the law, because she hath not performed the commandment of the king Ahasuerus by the chamberlains? And Memucan answered before the king and the princes. *Vashti the queen hath not done wrong to the king only, but also to all the princes, and to all the people that are in all the provinces of the king Ahasuerus.* For this deed of the queen shall come abroad unto all women, so that they shall despise their husbands in their eyes, when it shall be reported, The king Ahasuerus commanded Vashti the queen to be brought in before him, but she came not. *Likewise shall the ladies of Persia and Media say this day unto all the king's princes, which have heard of the deed of the queen. Thus shall there arise too much contempt and wrath.*

—Esther 1:15–18, emphasis added

There is a very significant lesson to be learned from Vashti, the First Lady of Persia and *Media.* Although the king's request may have been crude or even inappropriate, the real issue was not in what the king requested—the issue was how Vashti handled his request.

The Bible says in verse 10 of the first chapter of Esther that the king had commanded his chamberlains to bring Vashti before him to show the people and the princes her beauty. Some Bible scholars conclude that he was actually asking for Vashti to dance naked before his guests so that they could see what a fine wife he had! However, it is interesting to note that the inappropriateness of his request is not discussed—just the manner in which it was handled.

The Bible says that a woman who causes shame to her husband is "as rottenness in his bones" (Prov. 12:4). Ladies, you do not ever want to embarrass, shame, or disrespect your mate or any other man of authority publicly, especially as the First Lady or as any other ministry role. Why? Because the Scriptures show us that you are setting a precedent in your church and in the kingdom of how women will relate to their men. Like it or not, the First Lady is a position that women will imitate and emulate. You will be held accountable for what the women of your congregation see in your submission, how you talk to your husband, and in your general attitude.

All women have the power of persuasion. Vashti could have successfully handled this situation differently, by at least coming to the king and pleading out of the godly influence that God has given all women. Search the Scriptures and see how, from Genesis to Revelation, women have persuaded men. Eve persuaded Adam to do something God Himself told him not to do, and Adam was not confused about God's direction. Delilah persuaded Sampson after countless times of being tricked (you would have thought he would not have fallen for that one!). Esther persuaded Ahasuerus. The persistent woman in Luke 18:1–8 persuaded the judge. Mary persuaded Jesus to turn water into wine when He told her, "Mine hour is not yet come" (John 2:4). Our Lord and Savior was persuaded by a woman! So, ladies, use your God-given power.

Unfortunately, Vashti chose to have a poor attitude, walk in the flesh, and show the king that he did not control her.

It cost her the throne, her destiny, and her calling. The cost of a bad attitude can be very high!

If you have the Word of the Lord in you, and if you have any kind of relationship with the Lord that really matters to you, then you will do anything to stay connected to God.

Paul the Apostle said, "I will let nothing separate me from the love of God." Nothing means nothing! It means that you will not tolerate someone mistreating you; you will not put up with someone hurting you; you will not allow any devil from hell to get you out of God's presence and prevent you from being righteous before Him.

THERE IS NO SUCH THING AS A FIRST LADY WITH A BAD ATTITUDE.

You must remember that as a First Lady and co-laborer with your spouse, it means something to be a watchman over the souls of God's people. God will not allow you to continually abuse or mislead His sheep. Did not God ask Saul of Tarsus: "Saul, Saul, why persecutest thou *me*?" (Acts 9:4, emphasis added)? Saul did not touch the Lord physically, but in touching His children, he was persecuting God.

If your attitude is bad, it cancels you out from walking in this calling. There is no such thing as a First Lady (who is really one) with a bad attitude. We have a lot of women who want to climb up the spiritual ladder of success, who think they are ready to pastor, or ready to preach the gospel, but it first begins with your self-examination.

Being the pastor's wife, a pastor, or in any position in ministry is a "fish-bowl" lifestyle. There is no room for mistakes. You may ask, "How can I be this perfect person?" I know it is impossible to be perfect (even though we "strive" for perfection), but if your attitude is right, people do not always expect perfection from you. When you are arrogant, you make people beat you up; you make people talk about you. People look to find things wrong about you, just because of your arrogance.

Your attitude is often reflected in how much you smile. I believe that most women who do not smile are arrogant or they have some "head" (psychological) problems. I believe if other people are not smiling, you ought to give them yours. A smile disarms a lot of people. The prettiest smile ought to be on the face of the First Lady. Even if you have a grumpy husband, if you maintain a smile, the people will think, "He can't be so bad—look at his wife!" However, if both of you are grumpy, people will be afraid to approach you. When you think about how many people are dependent upon you to fulfill the role of a godly, caring, loving, supportive person, and how you can mess up that image, you will find the reserve and intestinal fortitude to reach down and grab a smile—even when you do not feel like it. You can find joy because you are a child of God and because you are responsible for setting the precedent.

My first wife, Denise, and I had some of our worst arguments before we got to church and then after we left out of church. That "last-word" demon will show up in the mouth of an immature person (both male and female), I promise you. When your attitude is bad, you will think first and last about yourself. You will not even care what people's opinions are about you. However, when you are in ministry, you live and die by public opinion.

You may say, "Well, I don't care." That shows signs of pride, immaturity, and irresponsibility. You do not need to be in ministry. You will not go far nor be successful in anything with that kind of attitude.

WHEN YOU COME INTO GOD'S
PRESENCE, YOU CANNOT STAY
THE SAME; YOU CANNOT
CONTINUE TO SIN AND
DISPLEASE HIM.

You need an attitude check every day. Not selfishness, but selflessness is the order of the day. It is not hard when you are a true servant of God.

An irritable attitude reflects a lack of a prayer life. You cannot convince me that you have any kind of decent prayer life or that you are in the face of God daily, when you consistently have such an ugly disposition. When you come into God's presence, you cannot stay the same; you cannot continue to sin and displease Him. You cannot stay before God and He not deal with you. Anybody that is mean, unfriendly, cantankerous, and critical and claims to have a word from the Lord, emphatically letting you know about the hours they spent in prayer, is a liar!

All of us have issues in our lives that are unpleasant. Mature people know how to handle daily dilemmas without bringing everybody into their conflict.

A First Lady must be so careful because, regardless of how anointed your husband is, your attitude can destroy everything God is trying to build. If you love God, you should never do anything negative, especially in terms of embarrassing your husband. (Remember Solomon said, in Proverbs 12:4, that a woman embarrassing her husband is like rottenness in his bones.) You should never do anything that would embarrass your husband publicly. You cannot ever justify that. Never! (Remember Vashti?) Neither can a man be justified in embarrassing his wife in public, for that matter. Neither of you should ever disrespect one another in a public place and justify why you had to "go off," bringing humiliation to the house of God, to the call of God, and to the Word of God. You cannot justify it one bit!

You must understand that you have one chance to make a first impression. If you lose that image of being a godly First Lady, it will be like letting go of feathers on top of a mountain and trying to retrieve them. The positive image of you will be gone forever. Think about some well-known First Ladies in ministry whose images have been tarnished; see if they can ever be respected as godly First Ladies again. Never. Ever.

When you really love God, you ask Him before you do or say anything: "Lord, will this hurt the church? Will this hurt the saints? Will I hurt You if I do or say this?" When you really love God, there are things you do not stoop to do because of the place you are in. "To whom much is given, much is required" (Luke 12:48, paraphrased). First Ladies are given much authority, much power, many benefits, and honor. You cannot forget that the flipside of all of that is a requirement of much sacrifice, much dying to self, much humility, much wisdom, and much patience.

———————— ~ ————————

> WHEN YOU REALLY LOVE GOD,
> THERE ARE THINGS YOU DO
> NOT STOOP TO DO BECAUSE OF
> THE PLACE YOU ARE IN.

I travel across the country and what I see in terms of First Ladies stinks! It seems as if no one is talking to these ladies about their attitude.

Now, I know some of you ladies out there may be thinking about now that, "Of course, as a man, you are just seeing one side." I do want to acknowledge another side to the First Lady dilemma: a common reason for First Ladies with bad attitudes is unsupportive husbands. I say to the men in my fellowship, "When you mess with my wife, you are messing with me." My former wife, Denise, was co-pastor, but even if she were not co-pastor, I would still tell them, "You are messing with me." If someone has a problem with my woman, come talk to me; but do not get up in my woman's face and do not even think about disrespecting her.

Sadly, many women do not have the support they need from their husbands. Could it be that the husbands are jealous of the call on their wives' life? Could it be that she is more disciplined to pray, to fast, consecrate, and study the Word of God? Could it be that she has the mouth of wisdom? Could it be that the husband may not like the attention the wife is getting in the church? Could it be the obvious, that the wife is the most anointed and so more people show up to listen to her than the pastor? I have to admit that, unfortunately, I have seen all of the above scenarios. Countless times, quite frankly, there has been a greater anointing on the woman of God than on her mate, and it usually results in a negative attitude in that woman, unless she is mature, steadfast, and grounded in the Word of God.

If you are a woman in this type of situation, let me tell you: you still have a responsibility to remain godly and not allow the kingdom of God to be blasphemed because of you. I recognize that this is a very hard situation. However, you must understand that through your blamelessness before God, He will be able to work on your behalf and He will fix the problem. If you allow yourself to have anxiety, become frustrated, and act out of character, you have then disqualified yourself from the divine intervention of God. But, when you remain blameless, your assured victory is in store. (See Proverbs 11:6.) To believe that anyone can keep you from your purpose and destiny in God is to place them at a higher level than God. As long as you obey what He says, know that your purpose will be fulfilled!

The growth of my church in the early years was due largely to my wife. She was visibly out front, and other women looked at her and said, "That's what I need to be like." I am extremely blessed by how God used Denise in that way.

Was Denise a perfect woman? No. She was not perfect. You are not going to live a perfect life, but you had better be striving for it. People know when you are trying, sisters. Part of your attitude ought to be humility. It is nice to be important, but it is more important to be nice.

Isaiah 1:19 says, "If you are willing and obedient, You shall eat the good of the land" (NKJV). This denotes more than just your physical actions of obedience. It emphasizes that both the action and the attitude are necessary for you to obtain the "good success"—the perfect will that God has for your marriage, your ministry, and your money.

Even as God may have blessed all of these areas in your life, when you look into the mirror of God, you better not begin to see yourself as a hotshot or somebody just so anointed above the rest. Do not allow people, things, accolades, or notoriety to mess you up. People can start whispering things in your ear and, before you know it, you start thinking you are who the people say you are. Never forget this very important fact: the same people who said, "Hosanna," a couple of days later said, "Crucify Him."

Your name, your gift, your connections, or your good looks may get you through the door, but only character will keep you there. You can teach what you know, but you will produce what you are. People will come to your church because of what you project; but when they ultimately see what you are, they will leave. Nothing will send people out of the door quicker than seeing a First Lady who is arrogant and whose attitude stinks. I know several pastors whose churches have emptied out because of the bad attitude of the First Lady.

Keep your attitude in check by maintaining a consistent prayer life and staying in submission to your husband. Your attitude will also stay in check if you submit yourself to other godly women who have gone through what you have to go through and who have been examples of virtuous women.

Most of us do not like being accountable to other people because we really do not want to be corrected. Every First Lady needs another seasoned First Lady to teach her to be sober, to love her husband, and to love her children. (See Titus 2:3–5.) Note that Paul acknowledged that there are some things that women need to teach women.

We all too often consider our friends to be the people who agree with us and tell us all good things, while the people who God sent into our lives to tell us the truth become the enemy. You need to find yourself a real friend—a woman of God that will teach you and train you like Naomi schooled Ruth. Your submission to a woman such as this will lead you right into your place of prosperity, peace, and provision.

REMINDER

Your attitude is the forerunner of who you really are as a person. Your attitude will determine the quality of relationships you will have in life, period.

CHAPTER 5

APPEARANCE

Now it came to pass on the third day, that Esther put on her royal apparel, and stood in the inner court...

—Esther 5:1

$\mathscr{A}$s a First Lady and as a leader that represents the authority of God, it is imperative that you understand what Esther understood about her role as a First Lady. Since you are the chosen and very elect of God, you have a higher level of expectation, sacrifice, and commitment that must be demonstrated, not just in prayer and consecration, but also in your appearance. You see, you too are in the "inner court" of the King. You represent His headship and His authority, and there is royal apparel that accompanies the inner court.

WE HAVE A RESPONSIBILITY AND ACCOUNTABILITY TO REFLECT MODESTY, INTEGRITY, TEMPERANCE, AND HOLINESS, EVEN IN OUR DRESS.

All throughout Scripture, there are indications of the importance of the garments worn by the priests and those in positions of authority. God commissioned Moses to sanctify the garments of Aaron and his sons. Esther knew to wear her royal apparel in the inner court. When Joseph was promoted to second in command, Pharaoh immediately "arrayed him in vestures of fine linen" (Gen. 41:42).

You must understand that just as in the days of old, your attire prophesies to your authority. Beggars wore the garments of beggars; whores the garments of whores; and queens, the apparel of royalty. Today, it is a travesty that we do not recognize the significance of our garments as men and women of God. We have a responsibility and accountability to reflect modesty, integrity, temperance, and holiness, even in our dress.

Understand that you are dealing with a very critical public. Although we cannot live our lives to please men, we are nonetheless charged not to offend those who are weak. Therefore, we must use wisdom concerning our dress, basing it on our audience. For example, wearing a pantsuit to a speaking engagement to minister would be something that you would need to know will not be an offence to your audience. Also, being overly "flashy" or overdressing may cause a schism and set a poor example for the other women in the church.

First Ladies, in particular, should be careful about their dress, because they are the trendsetters among the women in the church. Whatever "look" the First Lady sets will be the "look" of the entire church. If the First Lady starts whacking her hair off, you will have a church full of shorthaired women. If the First Lady wears pants to church, then so will the rest of the women. Women look to the First Lady to determine the standard or norm. Therefore, you must be particularly careful not to wear clothing, makeup, or jewelry that appears carnal and inappropriate for a church setting.

I have been appalled while going across the country and seeing the apparel of some of the First Ladies. Even the world understands that a dress code is necessary to maintain a professional environment. Do you not know that there is a certain dress code that must be maintained to keep a holy environment?

Some of what I am referring to relates to just being a lady. My mother would tell my sisters to take precautionary measures not to expose themselves or their undergarments if they are wearing a low-cut top. Under those circumstances, she taught them to put their hand over their chest if leaning forward. It is all about having tact, having poise, and having charm. Why, because you are going to produce after your own example. So, you cannot wear anything and everything.

You must be honest with yourself. If you are large in a certain area, be honest with yourself. Too many ladies are in denial. When you wear clothes so tight that they look like they are sprayed on your body, you are in denial. When any part of your clothing brings attention to any specific part of your body, you are inappropriately dressed. You do not want to bring attention to yourself because then the Christ that is inside of you is being overshadowed by your appearance.

A First Lady should never be caught with splits that are all the way up her dress or with cleavage showing. Just look at the First Lady of our nation and get a revelation of the importance of dress. You will never see the First Lady in anything remotely inappropriate. Why? Because she knows that her office demands respect and what she wears is a reflection of her position.

Another aspect of your appearance is not just your dress, but also your countenance. Although I have already addressed attitude in chapter two, I thought it must be reemphasized that your appearance includes your countenance, which is defined as *expression*. The look on your face, whether it is one of joy or the lack thereof, is just as much a part of your appearance, if not the most important part. As with the clothing, the precedent that you set with your countenance will be the standard of your church.

As a leader and as the leading example to the women of God, you must demonstrate the fruit of joy in your life. Dress codes were once enforced in the church as a religious constriction to enslave women. In response to these constrictions, we now see rebellious dressing in the church. At one time, pantsuits were not allowed in the church. However, there is nothing wrong with pantsuits. Unless the pants fit too tightly; then it becomes a stumbling block for some men. Tastefully appropriate is to have your jacket cover your derriere.

As a leader and as the leading example to the women of God, you must be a demonstrator of the fruit of joy in your life—even in your appearance.

REMINDER

Ladies, God doesn't want you to look like Hollywood, neither does He want you to look like you've been hauling wood!

CHAPTER 6

FAMILY

The heart of her husband doth safely trust in her... Her children arise up, and call her blessed.

—Proverbs 31:11, 28

*G*od is a family man. The whole creation began as a family and it is going to end with family. God created the family as the natural representation and vehicle by which we gain our revelation, appreciation, and definition of love, support, respect, authority, obedience, and character. It is the family that forms the community and church; and the communities formulate cities; and the cities make up nations.

It is the responsibility of the woman of the house to ensure that she *builds up her house*, and creates an environment that is healthy, productive, God-fearing, and loving. The woman is the critical component of every house and as it is in the natural, God utilizes the biological family to show us the spiritual parallel of His divine order.

The First Lady is also the God-ordained "builder" of the spiritual house. Building up the house refers to making sure that everything and everyone, every activity and every person within the house is in alignment with building or edification, construction, and positive development.

The Bible clearly states that, "Every wise woman buildeth her house: but the foolish plucketh it down with her hands" (Prov. 14:1). So, we know that any woman, any First Lady that does not edify her husband, her children, and any others that make up her house is a foolish woman and will destroy the house with her own hands.

The same principle applies to the First Lady as the builder of her church. As the "mother" of the house, you are more sensitive in many areas to the needs of the house than your spouse. The First Lady must perpetuate family. I believe this is the First Lady's main responsibility in the house of the Lord—to make sure the holistic family is ministered to.

Furthermore, I believe it is the First Lady's job to institute some ministries in the church to which the man just does not have the sensitivity or the wisdom. It is the First Lady that makes sure there is a nursery. What does a man know about having Pampers and toys in stock? It is the First Lady's job because she is a mother and she knows the needs of the family. She knows things the man does not and thinks about things that he does not.

For example, when trying to decide where the nursery should be in your beautiful new building, your spouse may choose the room in the back of the church by the exit door.

However, the First Lady would know that that room would not suffice, because of the draft coming through the door and the effect that the draft would have on the children, creating susceptibility to colds, flu, and other ailments.

It is also important that the First Lady does not have the attitude of a doormat (someone everyone steps on). The First Lady needs to speak up and not just be a knot on a log or just "the pastor's wife." The First Lady brings value to the importance of making sure holistically that every facet of the church appeals to each specific part of the family. She must have sensitivity for the men, women, and children.

Let's look at 1 Timothy 3:1–2 (NKJV) to get a clear picture of how God utilizes your family life to determine your ability to qualify for the spiritual parenting of His people:

> This is a faithful saying: If a man desires the position of a bishop, he desires a good work. A bishop then must be blameless, the husband of one wife, temperate, sober-minded, of good behavior, hospitable, able to teach.

It is quite clear that God utilizes one's everyday lifestyle, family structure, and marriage as a prophetic symbol and barometer of their readiness to oversee His house. The principle message of this scripture is that the way we live daily in our homes as spouses, and our ability to rule our houses and our children speaks volumes about where we are in God with relation to the level of maturity, wisdom, and responsibility that also comes with such a position of authority.

As the apostle Paul was talking to men, he was also

outlining the responsibilities of the First Ladies. How do I know this? Because some of the key elements that must be in order, such as having children in subjection and being given to hospitality, are usually responsibilities and giftings that God has placed within the woman.

The mother of every house, whether natural or spiritual, must have a real presence in order for that house to have the order that God has ordained. A mother's heart must be in the house of God to bring balance. This is also what Paul is saying to the First Ladies: help out your husband in the area of being patient, so he won't be a brawler. How many husbands have wives who will pull them to the side and say, "Honey, don't do that; don't say that." This is what a wife does. This is also what the First Lady should do.

You can tell when the First Lady does not have a voice in the church. In a ministry where the First Lady has a voice, there is balance, sensitivity, and creativity in the church. If the husband is not careful, he will have everything so regimented that the women many times will not be able to relate nor have an outlet to be the creative vessels and builders that God has called them to be. She will not have the freedom to be ministered to on the level that is necessary to grow, mature, and become whole. There are instances when the children will suffer along with the mother. It will eventually spill over to the church and cause the church to die out, because the pastor lacks sensitivity to the youth and does not recognize the changing of the times.

As the First Lady and the "Role Model Mother" of the church, the image that you project will be the image that you will draw. If you project an independent, non-submissive, cantankerous wife and mother image, you will draw the same type of individuals to your ministry. You will be held accountable by God for the image that you project to His sheep.

The First Lady (or co-pastor, etc.) must be submissive and understand parameters. If you do not understand these areas, you should not be in ministry.

Spiritual authority says that the man is the head of the house. The wife is the builder, but the husband is the head. Now, I do recognize for some spiritual houses, the order may differ; but regardless of titles between a husband and wife, at home the man is the head! God really does not use anyone who does not follow orders, because this would set the precedence of disorder and unruliness in a house. Since the wife sets the precedent in the house, you have a greater level of responsibility and the greater condemnation.

I must stop here to say this: as much as you have a responsibility in the church, your first responsibility is with your family. Often as ministries grow, husbands and wives begin to neglect one another and their children in the effort of trying to be successful in ministry. It is important to always remember, according to 1 Timothy 3:1–7 (paraphrased): "Your family's success precedes your ministry's success—when you do it God's way." You are a wife first, then a mother, and lastly a First Lady.

Many First Ladies make the mistake of forgetting they are married first. Whether the cause of abandoning the marriage is the church or the children, neglect of your spouse is wrong. If you have not prepared his dinner, or your home is nasty, or you did not make love to him last night like you promised, or things that he asked you to do are not done, or you drove all of the gas out of his car, or you did not make the bank deposit because you did not have time—honey, you are out of order! Take care of your man and do not take him for granted. Say, "Honey, is there something I need to do? Am I missing something here?" Make sure the needs of your spouse are being met.

I owe a lot to my first wife, Denise, in learning about myself and realizing my own needs. You would be surprised, ladies, what an impact your support, love, and kindness will do for your mate. I learned from Denise what kind of man I am. And in the process of her love, she showed me she was the one I needed. She was my cheerleader, and clearly admired me as a man. People all across the country would say to me, "I just love to watch your wife when you are preaching. She just sits there and smiles. She really loves you." I needed that. It spoiled me through the years, but it taught me that I needed someone who loved me and admired me.

We need First Ladies today that are going to learn how to admire their husbands again. Ephesians 5:33 says, "And the wife, see that she reverence her husband." To reverence means to be in awe of, to revere, to respect, and to pay homage to. God says for you to see to it that you do this. There are too many First Ladies and women in ministry who do not recognize the importance of admiring their husbands. It does not just impact him tremendously, but it impacts your children, the house of God, and, also, whether or not the church grows.

There are many women in ministry with issues against their husbands. Trust me, ladies, that issue will eventually come out of your mouth as well as be obvious in your body language. It is going to come out in the way you do not support him. People can tell when a husband and wife love, honor, and respect one another. It is the little things, and "the little foxes, that spoil the vines" (Song of Sol. 2:15).

Ladies, please understand how much of an important factor you are in the growth of your mate and in the growth of the church. As your spouse is inspired to do more for God, it is helpful when he receives your encouragement from home to be more anointed. Ultimately, the congregation becomes the recipients of that anointing. The people will be blessed, and be taught; they will receive their deliverance and grow by leaps and bounds. This will cause your ministry not only to grow but, more importantly, to be effective. So, if I know this, I know Satan knows this too, and he must not be allowed access to destroy what God is trying to build.

I know what some of you are thinking: "Apostle Turner, you do not know who I am living with! I cannot find anything to admire about him right now." Well, I say to you that you are going to have to "[call] those things which be not as though they were" (Rom. 4:17). I know it is not easy and it takes endurance. Yet, the reality of your relationship with God is that no matter how bad you believe your spouse is, when you go to God, He is always going to show you that the problem is not your spouse—it's you!

Some of you may have a hard time admiring your husband because you are so angry with him. You still haven't gotten over the summer of 1942. If that is the case, you have now entered into areas of pride, which leads you to become bitter. And, eventually, if you are not careful, the bitterness "dries the bones" (Prov. 17:22)—in other words, cause sickness and disease—and hand you over to death! So, for your own good, you must put away your pride, anger, and unforgiveness. You must see your husband as God sees him, love him unconditionally, and build him up.

> YOU CANNOT BE IGNORANT
> OF SATAN'S DEVICES. YOUR
> BATTLE BEGINS AND ENDS IN
> YOUR HOUSE.

For many of you, it is this same unforgiveness, anger, and disappointment that prevents you from submitting to your spouse. Well, I am telling you right now that you have already cancelled your date with destiny, unless you can walk in forgiveness. It is important to love your husband unconditionally, and if nobody else admires him, he needs to know that he has your admiration.

Satan knows that if he can tear up your marriage, he can also destroy your family, which will then bring destruction to his ultimate enemy—the church. You cannot be ignorant of Satan's devices. Your battle begins and ends in your house. This is why the enemy fights your marriage, tooth and nail. He particularly fights your marriage bed—the place of restoration, procreation, and (in Jesus' name!) recreation. Have you taken a look at the statistics of Christian marriages lately? Did you know that the divorce rate among Christians is higher than that of the world? Have you heard about the countless divorces among the five-fold ministry officers?

Now, allow me to give you a simple test of your marriage. This is the test: What is the state of your marriage bed? It's as plain as that. If you were to tell me the state of your marriage bed, I can tell you the state of your marriage. You say there is no marriage bed? I say there is no marriage. You say you have a great marriage bed? I say you have a great marriage.

Through a successful sex life God has designed that you and your spouse not just bond physically, but emotionally as well. That is why Solomon warned men that physical relations with women other than their wife would destroy their own souls. (See Proverbs 6:32.) What makes up the soul? The soul is made up of your mind, your will, and your emotions. So, what does frequent bonding with the husband produce? It produces a couple that not only becomes physically one, but a couple that starts thinking alike, finishing one another's sentences, and being of one accord. How do you develop this? It is not in the spirit, sister; it's in the bed.

Once again, that is why the Bible says that when a man has sex with a woman outside of marriage, he destroys his own soul. When a man makes love to a woman, he is releasing things not only out of his body, but also out of his mind, out of his soul, and out of his spirit. Could the lack of coming together be the reason why you and your spouse are not of one accord? God has fixed it so that you are the only person who can legally tap into the fullness of your mate's anointing. This is an awesome state of being, by which you are enabled to fully help your husband.

God also uses the marriage bed to replenish your energy. This is why I believe more than anything that every pastor (whether male or female) should be married. Why? Because your place of prayer (particularly with men) and your coming together with your spouse strengthens you. When a man is properly encouraged, loved, affirmed, liked, and admired by his wife, there is nothing he feels he cannot do. When the opposite occurs, there is nothing he feels he can do. I believe that the bulk of refreshing and inspiration is, yes, at the feet of Jesus, and the rest is in the marriage bed.

Satan has cleverly utilized his knowledge of the power of the marriage bed to get couples to argue, fight, and remain separate. The first thing that suffers is their intimacy. Quite frankly, I have encountered too many First Ladies who, because of their immaturity and lack of wisdom in this area, have made their husbands open prey for the devil. Although their "holding back" on their husbands did not give their husbands an excuse to sin, I believe that God also holds the wife accountable for being rebellious and clearly defying God's commandment concerning husbands and wives: their bodies no longer belong to themselves but to each other. We must not withhold our marital responsibilities from one another. Read 1 Corinthians chapter 7. There is no real reason to justify denying your spouse. Do you have an affectionate husband? If you do, he demands attention. God has placed you with that man to take care of him, love him, and support him.

You cannot be doing anything great in the kingdom of God if your house is neglected. Do not give the devil a place in your house, in your marriage, and in your children. I have seen an unfortunate number of wives who have not accepted their responsibilities for their families and are paying the price for their lack of sensitivity to their family's needs. Too many wives are destroying their marriages and, ultimately, their families because they do not understand both the natural and spiritual implications of maintaining healthy and consistent intimacy with their spouses. The relationship between you, your spouse, and God affects the entire family.

Ladies, you are on display as a First Lady (or pastor) and not only are the people watching every move you make, but God holds you even more accountable as a teacher: "Thou that preachest a man should not steal, dost thou steal?" (Rom. 2:21). If you have the gift of prophecy and you are exhorting women to live for God, obey God, submit and praise God in spite of their circumstances; you better make sure that you are the first partaker of everything that you are exhorting the saints to do.

I was the overseer of a ministry for women. The women who headed that ministry would be on the radio telling women to submit and love their husbands. Yet, they were two of the meanest women I have ever met. It would knock my socks off listening to them tell women to do what they were not willing to do themselves. As their overseer, I had to address the situation and correct their constant badgering of the ladies in their audience. I also had to remind them of their responsibility to actively seek to live what they preach. When you have godly integrity, your words and your deeds match. If your words and your deeds do not match, God will not honor what comes out of your mouth!

Needless to say, my relationship with those women was over after that conversation. Their ministry did not last long, since their message was not valid. It was not invalid because the scriptures they quoted weren't true. Yes, they quoted the scriptures accurately. However, their ministry was not valid because there was no power behind the ministry: these vessels were operating out of the "letter" of the Word (or out of legalism), instead of the "spirit" of the Word. You can only get the results of the anointing when the Spirit has been allowed to have liberty in you.

Your children will also speak of your effectiveness as a mother and builder of the home. Of course, I am not saying that your family should or will be perfect. We all know that most of the time, the end is better than the beginning when raising children; furthermore, raising children will have its ups and downs. You must remember that because of your spiritual position, Satan wants to embarrass and destroy you. He knows how critical you are, and I cannot stress enough that you must not be ignorant of his devices. The enemy will always try to attack you at your weakest links, which are often your children, and sometimes your spouse and family!

I have nine children and, believe me, every day the enemy attempts to come through one of them or the other. Knowing that my wife's "Achilles heel" is her children, we have had to strictly monitor their associations, their activities, and their lives. My wife and I spend a lot of time on the road, and we have three adults that help us to chaperone and escort our children everywhere they need to go. Besides prayer and speaking the Word of the Lord over their lives, we have had to solicit the help of our families and the saints to ensure that they do not get lost in the shuffle and that their physical, emotional, and spiritual needs are being attended to and met.

The woman, as the builder of the house, must always take inspections of her children and determine: Are they respectful? Do they dress respectfully? Are they representing the principles that we teach? Are they courteous, responsible? Do they have a foundation of the Word built inside of them? As you teach, train, love, correct, and discipline your children, despite what bumps may occur along the road, in the end, they will "arise up, and call [you] blessed" (Prov. 31:28).

PEOPLE WHO VALUE THEMSELVES ARE GOING TO TAKE CARE OF THEMSELVES.

About now, I know you may be thinking, "Okay. I know what I am supposed to be to my husband; I know what my responsibilities are as a mother; but what about me? Am I not part of the family? Do I not deserve a rest?" Well, the answer is yes, you most certainly do! I always advise parents that as much as any husband and wife love their children, and as much as they love their family, they need to plan and take time for themselves. You need to come apart before you come *apart*!

Do not allow your family and the ministry to consume

you to the point that you are tired and cantankerous. It is hard to be spiritual when you are tired. Satan loves to attack tired people. You must, as a wife and mother, firstly value yourself and your role in your home and in the ministry. People who value themselves are going to take care of themselves. They take time out daily for quiet time. Set priorities in your ministry and know that you cannot accomplish everything in one day. Accept the fact that what worked last week may not work today. You will not last long in ministry if you do not know how to adjust. Do your best…and then you rest.

Do not allow family, friends, or the saints to make you feel guilty about your commitment to your family and yourself. No one has the right to demand that you not be a wife to your husband, a mother to your children, or value yourself. It would be sad life to have a great ministry, but never have a great home to go to when church is over.

Remember your spiritual mother, Sarah, who had a voice with her spouse. She was submitted to her husband, and she made sure to look out for her child.

> …like Sarah, who obeyed Abraham and called him her master. You are her daughters, if you do what is right, and do not give way to fear.
>
> —1 Peter 3:6, NIV

Purpose in your heart today to be a daughter of Sarah and do what is right!

CHAPTER 7

WITNESS

Giving no offence in anything, that the ministry be not blamed.

—2 Corinthians 6:3

WE ARE THE keyhole through which people see Christ. We must make sure that whatever we do, we are guarding our witness. Particularly as church leaders and members of the five-fold ministry offices, we have a responsibility to "die to ourselves" at an even greater level. This is because we will often set the precedent for our local church, cities, and for those of us with national and international influence, nations. Have you been guarding your witness in conversation, attitude, appearance, and associations? If you don't invite it, you won't have to entertain it!

There are many interpretations of what it means to "come out from among them, and be ye separate" (2 Cor. 6:17). This has been a much-debated topic. I am not advocating being reclusive, arrogant, and "holier than thou." (We all know that at times Jesus ate with sinners and did some very unorthodox things to spread the gospel.) So, let me begin by saying that I am not referring to such specific situations where we are clearly led by the Spirit of God to minister to, or interact with, people who may have questionable lives when I say, "Be ye separate." Yet, I am referring to our everyday, consistent lifestyle of associations, habits, attitudes, appearances, and conversations.

Paul said to the Roman church, "For the name of the Lord is evil spoken of among the heathen because of you" (**Rom. 2:24**). We must remember that we still do have accountability as representatives of Christ to "abstain from all appearance of evil" (1 Thess. 5:22) and to protect our witness as being people who walk in truth, love, and integrity.

As Christian leaders, unfortunately your congregation and people in your city will blame the church for your personal mistakes. You must keep this in mind as you make decisions that involve business associates and everything else that you do. You are what you hang around.

Some of you are suffering right now from innocently entering into some situations that you had no idea would blow up in your face and cause reproach for you, your family, your church, and ultimately the kingdom of God. You need to always keep in mind that the devil wants to embarrass the house of God. He is waiting to find something on you to go to God about. That is why he is called "the accuser of the brethren" (Rev. 12:10). He wants to be able to accuse you of evil, deception, wrong associations, and bad attitudes. You need to aspire to be like Jesus so that when the devil comes, there will be nothing found in you.

Apostolic wisdom says, "If you want to know what you look like, look at your friends. If you want to know what you are going to become, look at your leaders."

Galatians 5:19–20 says, "Now the works of the flesh are manifest, which are these; Adultery, fornication, uncleanness, lasciviousness, Idolatry, witchcraft, hatred…" Obviously, these are all things that should not once be named among us as Christians and, particularly, leadership. However, far too often, not only has one been named among the five-fold ministers and First Ladies, but all of the above!

Lasciviousness is living a lifestyle so carnal that people cannot see Christ because they are looking at so much of you. You can be lascivious in your conversation, your dress, and/or your priorities. I have experienced far too many First Ladies and pastors whose primary conversation was their latest shopping spree, their next shopping spree, or what they were believing (by "faith," of course) for God to do for them, which usually amounted to more of a personal focus than one on the kingdom. Of course, I am not saying that we are not to believe God for the best and for things we desire. However, the current trend has produced a generation of people who have really disguised the "American Dream" under the cloak of "faith" and have abandoned the Great Commission.

Faith for big houses, expensive cars, and six-digit incomes is common in the kingdom, but where is the hunger for souls and the outreach ministries? Too many conferences and events have been directed at getting the house packed and inviting speakers that can raise the most money. What happened to trying to reach the lost and ministering to the poor?

Decked out in St. John suits and five-carat diamonds, much of the "faith" of the Christian leadership has been extended toward the next Mercedes Benz and the next house. Has anyone stopped to think what kind of image and witness is being projected? Do you have any idea what kind of people you are attracting and the underlying motives of many of the people that are sitting in the church today? Things have their place, but they are not priority.

We must preach, teach, and exhibit a balanced gospel and keep Christ and His kingdom's purposes above our own purposes. Even the world understands this principle for their leadership, which is why the president and his family know they cannot flaunt their wealth; they must be discreet. They also know that they must be discreet in their associations. They cannot wear anything that they want to wear. The world seems to understand the concept of dressing for success, but the saints think, "That's bondage." No, that is wisdom, maturity, accountability, and responsibility.

Furthermore, anyone who is not willing or able to step up to this responsibility need not place themselves in any position of leadership or responsibility where people will be influenced by you or looking to your lifestyle as a role model. If you do not want to make those adjustments, you do not need to be in ministry.

The First Lady of our country understands that for her "witness," she cannot wear everything. Yet, I have seen too many sensually dressed First Ladies in the kingdom of God. Yes, you may be shapely and voluptuous, but tight and clingy cloths, splits, see-through blouses, and low-plunging necklines have no place on women in ministry. The First Lady should never be found in clothing that compromises her witness and disrespects her husband. Read what the apostle Paul said about how God would handle lasciviousness in 2 Corinthians 12:19–21.

I remember a story about a First Lady that attended a conference with her husband. The conference was for a few days and her husband was the main speaker. She never came to any of the meetings until the last night that they were there. On the last night of her husband's engagement, she came to service dressed in tight leopard pants with an attitude to match. Needless to say, the focus and topic of that evening was not the Word or the move of the Spirit; it was the audacity of the First Lady to not attend any of the services and then, when she did come, to show up looking like a hooker. Ladies, something as simple as your clothing can cause people to lose respect for both you and your spouse, and that is not worth the contentiousness that it may cause.

You also must be cognizant of the beliefs of the people to which you may be ministering. If it offends your brother, you should stay away from it. Today, it is common for many women to minister in pants. However, if the church or ministry group that has sponsored your engagement is offended by you wearing pants, you need to know that, honor them, and not be prideful about making the adjustment. Remember, it is not about you.

> YOU MUST REMEMBER THAT
> WE HAVE BEEN CALLED TO
> COVER AND NOT UNCOVER.
> IT'S A "COVERING" AND NOT A
> "COVER-UP."

The Bible instructs us not to offend our brothers and to stay away from things that would cause those who are weak to backslide. There are too many ministers and First Ladies who do not believe they need to make adjustments. Instead, they demand that everyone else adjusts to them.

I know many First Ladies who go around telling their husbands' business—not only First Ladies, but women in ministry. If that is you, sister, then you have become a tool of the devil, betraying the trust of your husband, leadership, overseer, or whomever God has placed in your life as a spiritual authority. The devil will make sure your commentary gets back to the person that you have talked about so that he can accuse you of causing "discord among the brethren" (Prov. 6:19) (which, by the way, is something that God hates). (See Proverbs 6:16–19.)

You must remember that you have been called to cover and not uncover. Praise in public; rebuke in private. Even if your mate upsets you before church starts, you must uplift him as a man of God whenever you are before the saints. This is not a cover-up; it is a covering. This is maturity and it is a representation of a wise woman.

Am I saying that you pretend problems are not there?

No. Am I saying you do not deal with those problems? No. I am saying that you must be in order by only submitting your problems to those who are the ordained authorities in your life, such as, your overseer—not your girlfriends or your shopping buddies.

It is very important that you protect the witness of the kingdom. Yet, not only do you protect the witness of the kingdom, but also you must protect the witness of your spouse, your family, and your ministry. Again, I must stress that I am not saying not to deal with the issues; I am saying to deal with them in an orderly, respectful manner, protecting your witness and the witness of the kingdom.

We must grow up as leaders and realize that "to whom much is given, from him much will be required" (Luke 12:48, NKJV). God requires sacrifice, accountability, and responsibility for His leaders. Your problems are never so important that you have the right to offend the people who look to you for leadership and maturity. Whatever you may be going through, you have a responsibility to keep your attitude, conversation, and actions pure so that you will not be an embarrassment to the kingdom of God. If you cannot do that, you are not ready for ministry. You cannot get so angry with people that they see you upset: you should not walk out of a service or "go off" on someone who may have done something to you. Why? Because doing so oversteps the boundaries of a leader and a person who has been chosen by God to be an example to His people.

Another mistake I have seen many women in ministry make is attempting to be friends with the saints in the church, which ultimately leads to compromising their witness. People tend to lose respect for you when they become common with you. All of us have personal issues or quirks that often will be misunderstood, judged, and criticized by the average Christian, which is why you need not have any average Christians in your inner circle. You cannot be naïve about this. I know you are trying to be nice and approachable, and you can be that and still use wisdom. Even the world tells you that familiarity breeds contempt. People lose respect for you the closer you get to them. They will begin to say and do things that they normally would not say or do. They will begin to see you as their "buddy," and, eventually, see you as being on the same level as they are.

There are people who want to get close to you only to get in your business. It is not because they want to serve you, or because God led them. Honey, they are just trying to get in your business. They want to know how much money you make, what kind of house you live in, whether your children are on the ministry payroll, etc. You must understand these things and know how to feed people with a long-handled spoon. Otherwise, you are going to experience some things that could eventually damage your ministry.

I must admit that I have not always adhered to this, and I have suffered the consequences. I have found that no matter what you are going through, you must keep yourself in check. I have taken people into my "bosom" that really never had the character to be there. I have had some very overwhelming circumstances that I am sure most of you would agree could make anyone snap.

I lost my first wife of twenty years. Then, I went through

a divorce. My leadership had begun to attempt to tear up the church while I was grieving. The church suffered from this as well as from many other issues. Needless to say, I was angry. During the course of all of this, I said some things that I regret saying. I honestly do not even remember all that I said and did, because I was so out of it during that season. Adding to the situation, I was surrounded by people with wrong motives, people that were immature, and people who were never ordained to be a part of my ministry—much less part of my inner circle.

I have come to realize now, however, that I really should not have been in the pulpit. I should have taken some time off. I should have allowed myself to receive ministry, instead of pressing myself to minister in my condition. I should have been surrounded by people with the character of Christ to love and cover. I plead with you not to make the same mistake that I did. Only surround yourself with the few because, trust me, there are only a few God-ordained people that have been raised up to help you.

If you are angry and upset (particularly wives angry and upset with your husbands) and you cannot play it off, then stay home. It is better for you to be at home and protect your witness, than to come to church. Everyone will know that you are upset. If you allow them to sense that you are angry with your spouse through your body language, you will start the rumor mill going. Next thing you know, you will have the "hoochies" who have gotten "the word of the Lord" that your mate should be their spouse, and it will be just a matter of time before you have other negative situations to deal with. Does this sound far-fetched? Do you know there are often women waiting in the wings ready to pounce on any inkling of what may look like trouble in your marriage or trouble in your church?

This same principle applies to your leadership. A public display of dissention among you or your leaders often sends signals to the Absaloms and the snakes that it is time to come together and attempt a takeover. Even though everything I went through was hard and my feelings were legitimate, God still held me accountable for my actions. And God will hold you accountable, no matter how much you believe that you have a right to feel like you do. Remember, your issues and problems are not more important than your witness.

There are four things that I advise all of my ministers to do:

- Stay away from controversial issues.
- Stay away from controversial people.
- Stay away from controversial places.
- Stay away from controversial things.

You may feel like this is bondage, but remember that you must not "give place to the devil" (Eph. 4:27). You must be aware that you represent Christ and the ministry. If you do not, the blame will surely fall on you.

REMINDER

You are part of a kingdom team, not a member of a college debate team!

CHAPTER 8

PATIENCE

But let patience have her perfect work, that ye may be perfect and entire, wanting nothing.

James 1:4

PATIENCE IS A virtue and a necessary ingredient in being effective in both ministry and life. Without patience you will blow up, give up, and fail to reach God's plan of destiny for your life, for the lives of your family, and for your ministry. Often, patience is an overlooked component of success in life. Faith alone is not enough. The Bible says, "Through faith and patience [you] inherit the promises" (Heb. 6:12). If your great faith is not coupled with great patience, your faith will eventually die out and discouragement will set in. You will become distracted and disappointed, and defeat is certain.

IT WILL BE YOUR PATIENCE THAT
WILL SEE YOU THROUGH YOUR
MARRIAGE AND THE UPS AND
DOWNS OF MINISTRY.

I believe that women are usually more adept at operating in patience than men are. Oftentimes ladies, you have been sent to help your mates in this area. You have been gifted with the power of persuasion. You must use it to help your mate wait and not jump too quickly to do things.

For some of you, your patience is necessary for you to successfully deal with issues in your marriage. Your spouse may frustrate you in many areas and you are justifiably waiting for growth in those areas. You have to remember that all that God spoke concerning your spouse, your marriage, and your family was true. But, you must also remember that "better is the end of a thing than the beginning thereof" (Eccles. 7:8).

Your patience will see you through your marriage and the ups and downs of ministry. It is also the key to seeing the development of your children, who have been taught, but right now may not be demonstrating the principles and training that you tried to instill in them.

I want to encourage you to "Let patience have her perfect work" (James 1:4). Remember that "let" is a term of permission. I have discovered that impatience and pride go hand in hand—like kissing cousins. So, it is going to be an act of your will to allow patience to settle in next to your faith. People who struggle with patience must pray to ask God for the grace to remain patient, and quit doing things in their own strength. "Be strong in the Lord, and in the power of his might" (Eph. 6:10). Then, after being patient, you just stand still and see the salvation of the Lord.

I believe that the story of Esther is, again, an example of the type of patience that is required to reach your destiny and to follow the plan of God. After being selected as one of the virgins to be presented to King Ahasuerus, the Bible says that the preparation process was one full year. All the time that Esther was inside the palace, she was hiding her ancestry and, certainly, had to have suffered some anxiety and trepidation about having her nationality hidden. She could have succumbed to the pressure, but she waited, had patience, and continued to follow the advice of her Uncle Mordecai.

Think about the full implications of this story. Esther had to hide "herself," her traditions, her preferences, her wants and desires for a season—for the sake of a nation. You, too, ladies, often—for a season—must hide yourself, your desires, your wants, and your preferences for the sake of the "nation" or people that you have been called to save, deliver, and set free.

Let's continue with the life of Esther. When Haman convinced the king to sign a decree to destroy all of the Jews, one can only imagine the fear and dread that Esther must have felt. However, she could not overact or respond foolishly (or out of her emotions). She took the time to get sound counsel from her spiritual mentor, Mordecai, and followed all that he advised.

In the face of what could have been a very tumultuous situation, Esther did not just run to the king, even though the Bible was clear that she had more favor than the other women. She waited, fasted, and prayed, before she entered into the presence of the king. This was only after she had taken the time to seek the face of the Lord. She waited until she had counsel. She waited until she had completed her spiritual warfare. God gave her a strategy both naturally and spiritually in that she put on her royal apparel. In other words, in addition to pulling down spiritual strongholds, the sister made sure she was "fine" when she came into the king's presence. And, she looked so good that she caused the king to offer her half of his kingdom!

Do you think she would have gotten the same results if she had heard the news about the decree, panicked, and then rushed into the king's presence? I think not.

Many times we have very pertinent and serious situations that should cause us to stop and seek God, receive godly counsel if needed, and do the necessary spiritual warfare before we make major decisions or fly off the handle. Too many times we do not allow patience to have its perfect work.

You may have situations right now that, perhaps, should cause panic or depression. Do not allow the enemy to lure you into making a hasty and potentially fatal decision. I am not necessarily talking mortality, but fatality to your marriage, or your business, or your ministry. No matter how serious the issue may be, like Esther, you must be patient, trust God, and watch Him not only bring you out, but bring you out on top! Esther not only saved herself, but the nation was saved and her mentor, Mordecai, ended up being in the second highest position of power.

Like Esther, God has a perfect plan waiting for your situation, but you will only see it if you allow patience to do its work.

CHAPTER 9

GENEROSITY

It is more blessed to give than to receive.

—Acts 20:35

$\mathcal{T}$HE MINISTRY IS no place for stingy people. A misery, selfish, and self-centered person will only frustrate the grace of God in ministry. There is unequivocally no place in ministry for such a person. We have to always remember that the moment our ministries and our lives serve our own purposes more than the purposes of God and others, we are no longer servants.

There are four major areas of giving that every woman in ministry must learn. They are:

- How to share her husband
- How to share her home

- How to share her money
- How to share herself

SHARING YOUR HUSBAND

If your husband is the pastor, he is the focus of the attention of the church. People do not always follow or understand couth. If you have a problem with people not addressing you or making comments like, "Who is she?" Or, when people speak to him but they do not speak to you, your generous spirit that is full of love and patience must demonstrate grace and dignity. You cannot have a chip on your shoulder or be so insecure that you do not understand that there may be legitimate reasons that people act as they do. Many times people are just in a hurry and do not mean to overlook you. You cannot take these things personally, but you will need to have the ability to graciously offer your husband's attention to others and the matters of ministry.

If you are an insecure or a jealous woman, you must ask God to help you overcome your insecurities. There will always be other, attractive women and all types of situations that will occur that can potentially make you uncomfortable. You, again, must overcome jealousy in ministry.

IF YOU ARE AN INSECURE OR
A JEALOUS WOMAN, YOU MUST
ASK GOD TO HELP YOU TO
OVERCOME YOUR INSECURITIES.

It is human nature that makes people gravitate to the leader. People will come seeking the pastor's wisdom and anointing. Though they may love and respect you, often they are really not there for you. Most of your church members were drawn to your church because of your husband. Therefore, there is a need to accept the time, responsibility, and commitment that it requires for him to build up the house of God. I must add that, although the pastor is usually the one to whom members want to talk, I advise all of the pastors under my apostolic covering to never counsel without their wives. It is just foolish in this day and time to ever open any door for the enemy to come in.

I have seen too many wives competing for their husband's attention. They were not willing to make the sacrifice that it takes, particularly in the growing years of the church, when one is properly building a progressive and thriving ministry. First Ladies, support your spouse's commitments as much as possible and be realistic about the time and energy that it takes for him to pour a sure foundation in people, build relationships, and properly communicate with and train leadership.

SHARING YOUR HOME

We already know that 1 Timothy 3:2 tells us that we are to be "given to hospitality." The First Lady plays a major role in the fulfillment of that scripture. A true wife will know how to properly care for her husband's guests.

In reality, this has nothing to do with being a First Lady; it is just plain good manners. You should greet the guests, making them feel comfortable and fulfilling any need they may have. Never make anyone feel uncomfortable or unwelcome in your home.

Your spouse may bring unexpected guests home with him. You may have had an argument with your spouse and unexpected guests show up at your door. Perhaps unexpected guests show up at your door that are really not unexpected, as you soon discover that your spouse forgot to inform you that he invited them. Your response in any of these events must be one of maturity, confirming the fact that you have become that gracious hostess that God has called you to be.

At least 200 of the 365 days in a year, company is in my home. I could not do that unless I had a wife who was generous enough to share our home. I am afraid of First Ladies who have never opened up their homes to anyone. Such behavior is indicative of a First Lady who has a social problem and may not realize it. I am not suggesting that you open your home to everyone or even to a lot of people, but I believe it is impossible to be very effective in ministry without having some level of intimacy with others. I am not referring to your congregation. I am referring to other leaders, like pastors, your overseer, or co-laborers with whom God has intended for you to fellowship.

Hospitality was one of the overlooked strengths of the church in the Book of Acts. Didn't the Bible say that they "went from house to house"? Again, in no way am I advocating that pastors or leaders interact with the sheep on that level or become co-dependent on any person. However, I do know that there is a place, a purpose, and power in such fellowship.

THE KINGDOM OF GOD IS TRANSFERRED THROUGH RELATIONSHIP.

I have often witnessed such gatherings being the opportunity that God uses for his leaders to be encouraged, restored, and delivered. So, you must understand that God uses these types of gatherings for His purposes. Do not look at them simply from a personal preference.

I believe that the most successful and effective leaders are relational. The kingdom of God is transferred through relationship. Elijah's anointing was transferred to his spiritual son, Elisha, through relationship. Moses and Joshua and Jesus and His disciples are also examples of transference of anointing through relationships—through all of those intimate moments and times of fellowship.

Whether you consider yourself an introvert or extrovert, a sanguine personality or a melancholy, allow the Holy Spirit to guide you and use you and your home to be a place of restoration, reconciliation, recreation, and rejuvenation.

THE FIRST LADY OUGHT TO BE THE LEADER IN THE CHURCH IN TERMS OF GENEROSITY.

SHARING YOUR MONEY

Look at the woman in Proverbs 31 who we know as the "virtuous woman." This virtuous woman is the prototype of every Christian woman. The giving she displays is a trait that should exist in every child of God— particularly those who are in ministry. Her generosity in giving to others is one of the recurring themes of this awesome woman in Proverbs 31. Verse 15 says that she "giveth meat to her household, and a portion to her maidens." Verse 20 says, "She stretcheth out her hand to the poor; yea, she reacheth forth her hands to the needy." It is clear that she takes care of her own house well, but it is just as clear that she also blesses those around her, as well as the needy.

The First Lady ought to be the leader in the church in terms of generosity. However, I have to temper what I am saying in order to bring balance. My wife, Denise, was small in stature, yet she was big in giving. She was the most giving person I have ever known.

Unfortunately, usually the biggest suckers for a sad story are those who have the gift of giving. I have not yet seen a person who had a gift of giving who did not have a mercy gift as well. Those two gifts run together, just like the power gifts (the gift of faith and the gift of healing) always go together.

I am not endorsing giving so much that you do it apart from wisdom, because that can cause problems. For instance, I would never give money to a woman unless I talked it over with my wife first; doing so would not be wise. Yet, there is something wrong in our hearts when we never deny ourselves or our ministry for the sake of others. There is a need now more than ever for the body of Christ to evaluate itself in the area of giving.

I had a preacher once tell me that God did not need his money, because God already had all of him. (I think God might be requesting an exchange on that one!) It is appalling to see the number of ministers who are cheap, yet these same ministers exhort the saints to live by faith.

I believe that how you handle your money is how you handle the anointing. I also believe that money is one of the faith tests that every believer must pass if God is really going to bless you at your greatest potential. Why do I say that? Let's just look in the Bible at the money tests.

Gehazi, who should have inherited Elisha's anointing, which was a double-portion anointing at that, failed the money test. He could not perceive passing up the things that Naaman had offered Elisha, and Gehazi sold out for material blessings. The issue was not that God did not want him to have these things. The issue was as the prophet asked him, "Is it not the time?" (**2 Kings 5:26**). God does have the best in store for us, but there is an appointed time for that vision to come to pass.

The person we refer to as the rich young ruler in Luke 18 led what most of us would probably consider an upright, moral, and righteous life. He kept the commandments from his youth. He went through the trouble of seeking Jesus, but we find out that his seeking would only be on his own terms. When Jesus let the young ruler know what it would really require to seek Him, the Bible says, "He was very sorrowful: for he was very rich" (v. 23). Jesus let this zealous follower know that there was still one thing he lacked (v. 22).

Unfortunately, there are many still today in the body of Christ who lack the same thing. Yes, you may pray. Yes, you may fast. Yes, you may feed the poor and come to church faithfully. The question is: have you really given God your all? Can you deny yourself that shopping spree or other luxuries and plant seed in another ministry? Have you turned over to Christ and the kingdom that area where your treasure is? Your treasures lead to the place where your heart dwells.

Many saints, when it comes to giving, do not trust God to provide for their needs. Could this be why statistics show that only 12 percent of the church really tithes?

I want to address tithing, because I believe tithing is very critical, particularly among leaders. I believe that church leaders should give a tithe outside of their ministries to their overseers, spiritual parents, missions, etc…to literally give to God what He requires. When ministers simply tithe to their local church, they are just giving back to themselves. True, it may go for the building project, but it is *your* building project. I know it does not go directly to you, but indirectly, it still benefits you. Therefore, I believe that we really honor God's tithe when we give outside of ourselves, to other ministries, and trust God to meet our needs.

Many times it is the woman who is the leader in giving in the home. Paul the Apostle took the time to note the key women that supported his ministry. Of the devout Greeks he said, "and of the chief women not a few" (Acts 17:4) aided in his ministry.

As the woman of both your natural and spiritual house, you must have a healthy, biblical perspective about giving, tithing, and sowing, in order for your house to flourish and continue in the blessings of the Lord. You may even have to help your husband in this area. Utilize the wisdom that God has given you.

Tithing and giving are so critical because through them God "will rebuke the devourer for your sakes" (Mal. 3:11). I have seen too many leaders struggle in their churches and in their homes for years and years and cry out to God, "What am I doing wrong?" Well, let's start with your tithes and offerings. Are you tithing to your spiritual leader? You teach others to tithe and honor their leadership, are you doing the same? I cannot tell you how many ministers I have encountered who are in this predicament, yet every dollar they get goes right back to themselves.

I must clarify that I do understand that when you are just starting your ministry you have to put every dime into what you are doing. Have you considered your personal income from your job or from your speaking engagements? You could tithe from those. Some people send their personal tithe to their local church and a church tithe to their overseer, or vice versa. Whatever God leads you to do, you must do it quickly so that you can begin to experience the never-ending supply that comes when you fully obey God and you hold nothing back.

Too many ministers have made their churches their treasure. They are so afraid of taking money from the church and they are so busy laboring over the next project that they have forgotten the principle that brought them thus far: "Give, and it shall be given unto you; good measure, pressed down, and shaken together, and running over..." (Luke 6:38).

Ladies, you are so vital to the success of this area in your home and ministry that I do not believe I can emphasize it too much. Getting the victory over stinginess, greed, overindulgence, and all the trappings that come along with ministry is often left to the hands of the woman of the house. In the Bible, Abigail understood this principle and saved her own life and the lives of her entire household because, though her husband did not see the need to give, she knew she had to respond to David's request. Abigail's wisdom and generosity saved many lives. (See 1 Samuel 25.)

FIRST LADIES SHOULD BE
WOMEN GIVEN TO GENEROSITY
AND INTEGRITY, HAVING
VICTORY OVER GREED.

You, too, may have some situations where pride and ego may prevent someone from wanting to give, but that seed sown may be the key to having life and having it more abundantly. You could be called to give to an enemy or someone not thought to be worthy, but you must hear God, obey Him, and live.

Lastly, I have counseled many ladies who have attempted

to abdicate their responsibilities in this area of financial integrity and tried to place it on their spouses. In Acts chapter 5, the story of Ananias and Sapphira teaches us that although the man is the head of the house, the wife will not be found blameless. Why? The Bible says Ananias "kept back part of the price, his wife also being *privy* to it" (v. 9, emphasis added). If you are privy to any lack of integrity in this area, you will be held accountable if you fail to do anything about it, or worse, go along with it. It is no coincidence that the first form of judgment in the New Testament Church involved money. You must be a woman given to generosity and integrity, having victory over greed.

Sharing Yourself

One of the key facets of ministry that follows the example of Jesus Christ, is our daily call "to die" and to deny ourselves. We have to be ever so careful not to get to the place of such comfort, success, and importance that we have stopped dying and stopped denying. When we get to that place, we have become arrogant, prideful, and no longer servants. We have to die to our own preferences, bad habits, and rude assumptions. We have to die to our own thought life, traditions, and lifestyle in order to line ourselves up with God's Word and His ways.

There will be times in ministry that God will call you to give yourself to others in such a way that seems unfathomable to others. Ruth had such a charge from God. Ruth was blessed in the end because of her total dedication and commitment to her mother-in-law, Naomi, who had no visible means of being a benefit to her. Naomi was widowed and broke, but Ruth gave of herself to Naomi, because she saw that Naomi held the spiritual impartation that she needed.

You may either be the "Naomi" giving impartations or the "Ruth" going out of your way to receive one. Either way, it requires you to come out of yourself, out of your comfort zone, and to totally submit your body, soul, and spirit to God and His purposes.

In giving of yourself, there will be times when you will have to comfort the feeble-minded. You will have to suppress your flesh and its desires in order to help, encourage, and even mentor people who you may not have chosen, if God had asked for your opinion. In mentoring them, you will have to hold their hands for a season.

I believe that after God has your money, your time, and everything you have on the altar, then you are the last thing He requires. As the leading lady, you must be the first partaker and the prime example of a life that has been totally surrendered to God and His kingdom's purposes.

I have been appalled at the lack of denial of self I have witnessed among men and women of God. We have begun to operate according to our feelings at an unprecedented level. We know that we are not giving of ourselves when we operate out of our emotions.

I believe one of the best examples of this type of behavior is in the movie, *The Preacher's Wife*, starring Whitney Houston and Denzel Washington. Whitney Houston's character, the First Lady, never prayed. She moved by her emotions and got caught up in her own selfish desires and fantasies. As a woman of God, you cannot be a purely emotional being. You will have emotions and emotions demand expression, but you must then submit your emotions to the Word of God and its power, relinquishing any anger, hurt, rebellion, discouragement, envy, jealousy, and desire to the Holy Spirit.

I would like for you to take a few moments right now to ask God to show you any areas in your life that you have not given totally to Him. After He has shown you these areas, please repeat this prayer:

> *Father, in the name of Jesus, I come before You today, asking that You forgive me of my sin of selfishness. I know that Your Word says that if any man desires to follow You, he must deny himself and take up his cross daily. Right now, Father, as I have repented of my selfish ambition and lack of self-denial, I commit to deny myself of anything that is not pleasing to You. I commit to humble myself to the correction of Your Word and Your Holy Spirit in every area of my life. I will deny myself the right to get even. I will deny myself of overindulgence. I will deny myself of my own opinions and submit all of my ways to You. I will be confident that You will direct, avenge, and establish me in all of my ways. Lord, I take up the cross that You have given me, the burden for souls, the purpose for which You have placed me here in this earth, and I leave everything else at your feet. I thank You, right now, Father, that*

Your grace is sufficient. I can rest in that because those that fear You have strong confidence. So, I now give You the praise, honor, and glory for the victory! Amen.

REMINDER

You love like you give; you give like you love.

CHAPTER 10

WISDOM

The fear of the LORD is the beginning of wisdom...

—Proverbs 9:10

$\mathscr{W}$E KNOW THAT "the fear of the LORD is the beginning of wisdom," so we begin our lifelong wisdom journey when we accept Jesus as our Lord and Savior and reverence Him as "the author and finisher of our faith" (Heb. 12:2). Therefore, I must begin this chapter on wisdom by emphasizing this very critical point:

"The fear of the LORD" is reverential respect and awe of God. I believe this is one of the key elements that are missing in our marriages, homes, and ministries. This is why many of us are not seeing the miracles, signs, and wonders as in the days of old. The fear of the Lord has diminished.

The Bible says that sound wisdom is laid up for the righteous (Prov. 2:7). The fear of the Lord, beloved, will stop you from compromising. It will keep you from doing or saying the wrong thing, from being around the wrong people, and from being in the wrong place at the wrong time. The pure and essential reverence of our Almighty God—who has the power to split every neutron and electron in our bodies, and can put both body and soul into hell—is missing today in the average church and among the average Christian and the average minister.

How can I say these negative things about the church? It is because of many of the abominable, irreprehensible words, thoughts, and activities that exist in the body of Christ.

Sadly, many of the attitudes, politics, and pervasive ideals are accepted in exchange for celebrity, fame, exposure, and money. There are just some things you would not wear, words you would not say, places you would not go, and actions you would not do if you really have the fear of the Lord. Let us take a look at what the Bible says about the fear of the Lord.

The fear of the LORD...

- is the beginning of wisdom (Ps. 111:10).

- is the beginning of knowledge (Prov. 1:7)

- prolongeth days (Prov. 10:27)

- is strong confidence (Prov. 14:26)

- is a fountain of life, to depart from the snares of death (Prov. 14:27)

- is the instruction of wisdom (Proverb 15:33)

- tendeth to life: and he that hath it shall abide satisfied; he shall not be visited with evil (Prov. 19:23)

- are riches, and honour, and life (Prov. 22:4)

The churches...walking in the fear of the Lord, and in the comfort of the Holy Ghost, were multiplied.

—Acts 9:31

So, it is an exercise in futility to emphasize wisdom if you do not have a real reverence for God, His Word, His omnipotence, and His power. Why? Because reverence is where true wisdom begins.

Many times it is my fear of the Lord that stops me from saying or doing hurtful things. I know God is loving and forgiving, but I also know that I will reap what I sow. I know God is good and merciful, but the teacher (and leader) will have the greater condemnation. I know God will forgive me and love me always, but I also know that as a man or woman of God in a place of authority, power, and experience, I can disobey Him and end up like Moses—unable to enter my promised land.

Do you have a healthy fear of the Lord that keeps your tongue from evil? Are you always aware that God hears every vow you have made and holds you accountable? Do you fear God enough to know that even if you do not open your mouth, you must daily die to the internal thoughts and activities of your heart that may displease Him? If you do not consciously and actively examine yourself, you do not have the fear of the Lord.

Those that fear the Lord have a hard time judging others, because they know that they are "a wretch undone." Those that fear the Lord do not want to offend Him in any way: not in dress, not in speech, not in actions, nor in associations. Those that fear the Lord inquire of Him and seek His approval and permission in every aspect of their lives. Those that fear God seek godly counsel, knowing that in the multitude of counselors, there is safety. Those who do not fear God make up their own minds and say, "God said it," masking their independent spirit with false spirituality.

I want you to take a few moments to ask God:

- Have I demonstrated total reliance on You in every area of my life?

- Have I demonstrated total reverence for You in my marriage, ministry, on my job, as a parent, in relationships, and with my money?

If you need to repent, take the time to do so, and ask the Holy Spirit to teach you how to "be renewed in the spirit of your mind" (Eph. 4:23).

———————— ∼ ————————

Now that you are sure that you have entered on the wisdom route through a healthy fear of the Lord, it is imperative that a spirit of wisdom guides you in all that you do.

To have a "spirit of something" means to have the breath, life-giving force, or disposition of something. So, when we operate in the breath and disposition of wisdom, it will bring forth life and health. This principle can be applied to our personal lives, relationships, businesses, and ministries.

The marriages and households that have this spirit of wisdom operating in them will be marriages and households that bring life and reflect the image of wisdom in all that is connected to them. Isn't that why Sheba was blown away with Solomon? The Bible says in 1 Kings 10:4–5:

> And when the queen of Sheba had seen all Solomon's wisdom, and the house that he had built, And the meat of his table, and the sitting of his servants, and the attendance of his ministers, and their apparel, and his cupbearers, and his ascent by which he went up unto the house of the LORD; there was no more spirit in her.

When she saw his wisdom, how he handled business, how he treated his people, how his servants were dressed, how he decorated the palace, how he was able to answer her questions, the girl fainted!

People should be able to "see" your wisdom, whether it is through how you raise your children, in your marriage, or in your ministry. Unfortunately, in today's commercialized society, if you followed home many of the people who are on television discussing their five-part series on areas of wisdom, you would have a hard time finding wisdom.

Make a commitment today that you will make wisdom the principle thing and pray for the spirit of wisdom, according to Isaiah 11:2. When you begin to operate from the spirit of wisdom, and not just simply applying wisdom here and there, your wisdom will be reflected in everything you do. Or, in other words, that spirit will have a seat within you, so everything you do will be processed through wisdom.

Where do I start? How do I operate in this spirit? If you have been reading this book with an open spirit, you are already on your way. As you continue to pray, seek the direction of the Holy Spirit, study the Word of God, and seek godly counsel, you will begin to make decisions that reflect the disposition of God as opposed to the disposition of your experiences, your opinions, and your preferences. Let me give you an example of the spirit of wisdom in action.

On many occasions, I have had to share some things with wives concerning their husbands (prophetically, pastorally, and psychologically). Please note, I am not referring to violating confidences of spouses or anything of that nature. I am specifically referring to cases requiring me to give both practical and biblical instruction to women who were married to "Nabal."

Now, the wives with a spirit of wisdom took what I shared with them as their spiritual leader, gave it to God, and were led by the Spirit of God on what to do and even what to share with their spouses, if anything. The foolish women often repeated everything I shared with them (which was only for their benefit) with "Nabal"—a fool.

Now, we know the Bible says that "fools despise wisdom and instruction" (Prov. 1:7). So, guess what happened? Most of the time, the fools got offended and angry, and usually the family—and then ultimately the marriage—was destroyed. In contrast, many of the wise women's marriages were redeemed. Often, the mate later got saved or delivered and their houses were set free.

So, what am I saying? Many times you, as the First Lady and the woman of the house, have to be very discerning of the Spirit of the Lord. I believe we would have more unity among the brethren if we had more women of wisdom. You see, even though your friend may have told you that "Bishop-know-it-all" made some disparaging remarks about your husband, if you really hear from God, it may not be wise to tell him. The Bible says, "A fool uttereth all his mind" (Prov. 29:11). You do not need to tell everything you know. Or, if your spouse hears some things that are disturbing to his male ego, you do not chime in and feed his anger. Rather, you speak out of a spirit of wisdom and love, encouraging him and reminding him of what the Word of God says.

Please note that the spirit of wisdom is not possibly in operation when a person's decisions, comments, or actions are in direct opposition to the Word of God. Below are some of what I consider to be the major areas of wisdom that need to be addressed among God's leading ladies:

WITHHOLDING SEX FROM THEIR SPOUSES, FOR WHATEVER REASON

Remember, there is no wisdom apart from the Word of God. I wanted to start with what is natural. The Bible warns us in 1 Corinthians 7:5: "Defraud ye not one the other, except it be with consent for a time...that Satan tempt you not for your incontinency." The same passage also mentions in verse 4 that the woman does not have power over her body, but the husband, and vice-versa. So, it is clear that the lack of a sex life will give place to the devil and open the door for adultery, perversion, and other types of sin.

Now, ladies, I need to keep it real right here. Most anointed men have a very strong sexual appetite. Can you say, "David?" David was a worshiper and a man after God's own heart. However, you can see by how he went after both Abigail and Bathsheba that he was still just a man, and when he saw a fine woman, he wanted her.

Just check it out in Scripture. Judah, Abraham, Sampson— all of them had a time in their lives where they justified their sexual satisfaction in a time of stress.

You do not want to have your husband in such a vulnerable position where he is stressed on his job, stressed at the ministry, and then, because he is not being fulfilled at home, stressed at home. Remember this simple equation:

STRESS + STRESS + STRESS = MISS—STRESS!

I cannot begin to tell you how many saved men of God have either fallen in this area or are struggling with great difficulty, often because of an insensitive wife that has convinced herself that her spouse is too saved to want sex. Please do not make this very unwise mistake.

PREACHING/TEACHING/COUNSELING FROM YOUR EMOTIONS RATHER THAN FROM THE SPIRIT OF GOD

Emotions demand expression, but emotions must be managed. We are all emotional beings by nature, but we must bring "into captivity every thought to the obedience of Christ" (2 Cor. 10:5) if we are going to be spiritual and walk in wisdom.

I have seen too many women (and, quite frankly, men as well) begin to teach and preach from what they call "revelation," but it is actually from the soulish realm where they have been wounded or hurt. For example, you may be going through a divorce, so because you are hurting and upset over your husband's lack of commitment or whatever may have been the problem, you do a ten-week series on "Husbands, Love Your Wives OR ELSE!"

Often, when we have been through traumatic experiences, such as divorce, betrayal, or loss, we really need to check and double-check with God to make sure that it is not our emotions, our hurt, and our resentment talking, as opposed to the Spirit of God. I have learned not to trust myself in times like that and stay away from those areas until I know that I can deliver a balanced, Spirit-influenced message, rather than voice my own frustrations under the guise of a sermon. Trust me. I have been there, and the result of preaching out of emotions is usually that you will offend, confuse, and possibly even scatter the sheep.

COPYING/MIMICKING OTHERS RATHER THAN FINDING OUT WHO YOU ARE AND BEING THAT PERSON PERFECTLY

One of the greatest examples in the Bible of a person knowing who they are and understanding their own strength is David. He was a shepherd boy, and he had been trained as such. When David was preparing to fight the giant, Goliath, Saul tried to put his armor on David. David soon realized that he could not fight with anyone else's armor. He had been trained to fight in the sheep field and he had to trust God that His grace was sufficient.

Have you ever been in the middle of a "fight" and realized you were trying to fight your battle with somebody else's armor and not your own? God has prepared all of us in our own particular fields and has showed us how to get victory in our battles. Some achieve tremendous results when they fast and pray for twenty-one days. God has trained them and revealed to them that this is their primary weapon of warfare. Am I saying that only some should fast and pray? Of course not. We all should have a lifestyle of fasting and prayer, but there are some saints whom God trains and prepares so that fasting and prayer is their primary weapon of defense.

For others, their weapon of warfare may be in the area of giving. My current wife, Darlyn, shared with me that when she was growing in the Lord her weapon was often her seed.

As she was going through major traumas and battles, God would challenge her to give a supernatural seed and, as a result, breakthrough would come to her. For Darlyn, giving is her primary weapon.

In whatever way God has prepared you, shown Himself strong in your life, and instructed you, you must be confident in how God has taught you how to fight. Don't try to put on somebody else's weapon because it sounds or looks more spiritual or sensational. Listen to the Spirit of God and be obedient to His instructions for your life.

I am convinced that too many people in ministry are walking around carrying Saul's heavy armor when all they need is a slingshot and five smooth stones. Mimicking others and trying to copy rituals, ministries, mandates, or visions that belong to others will only leave you feeling over burdened and paralyzed.

FAILING TO DEVELOP
KEY RELATIONSHIP SKILLS

The kingdom of God is transferred through relationship. Elijah's anointing and mantle was transferred to the person with whom he had the closest relationship. Samuel was mentored and trained through his relationship with Eli. Jesus had to spend three years with the disciples, night and day, in order to transfer the kingdom into their bosom. The disciples would not have been able to continue to advance the kingdom with simply a casual, polite, non-committed relationship with Jesus. They had to spend time with Him, walk with Him, observe Him in His "weakness," and put in the sacrifice that it takes to truly develop relationship.

There is an alarming culture of isolation among ministers and the body of Christ that hinders us all from benefiting from the skills and abilities of others. The types of relationships that build the kingdom require sacrifice of time and money, being inconvenienced, open to correction and instruction, and denial of fleshly motives and desires. Many times, the First Lady is key in bridging these types of relationships between ministers, churches, and families.

Take a look at the Shunammite woman in 2 Kings 4:8–11 (emphasis added):

> And it fell on a day, that Elisha passed to Shunem, where was a great woman; and *she constrained* him to eat bread. And so it was, that as oft as he passed by, he turned in thither to eat bread. And *she said* unto her husband, Behold now, *I perceive* that this is an holy man of God, which passeth by us continually. Let us make a little chamber, I pray thee, on the wall; and let us set for him there a bed, and a table, and a stool, and a candlestick: and it shall be, when he cometh to us, that he shall turn in thither. And it fell on a day that he came thither, and he turned into the chamber, and lay there.

This woman is a prime example of the woman of the house having the perception, insight, spirituality, and wisdom to be led by the Spirit of God to connect to right relationships. The Bible says in verse 9 that, "*she* perceived." She initiated a relationship with the man of God. There is no indication throughout the entire story that this woman's husband ever had much perception, spirituality, or understanding. She continued to be the one who stood in the gap for her child, believed the prophet, and actually was the obvious spiritual leader in her house. It was because of this woman's initiation of relationship with the prophet that she and her husband got their miracle.

Regrettably, there are too many instances where the First Lady is actually burning down these types of bridges because of her attitude, selfishness, or lack of understanding of the importance of relationships in ministry, business, and family. First Ladies, you are often the key to perceiving right relationships, but you must be able to discern and respond correctly to those whom God has " passing you by continually." I promise you, the right people are in your vicinity. Do you have the relationship skills needed to properly respond to those God has called you to reach out to?

No matter how successful you and your ministry may be, you have an "infirmity," and God has a relationship established for your infirmity. An infirmity is an area where you are not firm. So, you may have a 30,000 person congregation, but if your marriage is not firm, God has someone with the wisdom to help you and your spouse in your marriage. Or, maybe your marriage is fine, but you need wisdom in how to build your ministry. Whatever area you need help in, God has "a brother born for your adversity (Prov. 17:17). God lets us know that there is someone ordained to assist us in our adverse situations, but we have to be led by the Spirit of God and not so lifted up in pride that we do not want to get help. For God to say he has a brother born for our situation lets us know that the brother that has been raised up (or sister, of course) is the one anointed for that particular challenge in our lives. We often deal with situations too long and go through unnecessary changes because of our lack of relationship building and our suspicious attitudes, pride, and arrogance. Are not two better than one?

One of the reasons why many of us struggle with depression, anxiety, addictions, and guilt is that we failed to complete certain developmental tasks when we were growing up. The Bible clearly reveals how strongly God feels about the importance of relationships. God said, "It is not good that the man should be alone" (Gen. 2:18). Living in relationships, better known as "bonding," is the foundation of God's character, which is why God made us—He wanted a relationship with us.

Relationship is our most fundamental need. Without attachment to God and others, we cannot really be ourselves. Failure to bond in the past interferes with bonding in the present. People who never develop an emotional bond to anyone and remain disconnected fear that other people hate them or will hurt them.

People who do not make emotional attachments to God and others live in a perpetual state of not getting their needs met. We all have three primary needs: to give love, to receive love, and acceptance. Emotional detachment creates a deficit of the primary needs and, as a result, creates isolation. Isolation is very dangerous and is actually abusive. Ask a prisoner how it feels to be put in isolation. There are many ministers in isolation, some involuntarily, but most often voluntarily, due to their lack of developing relationship skills.

Let's examine three stages of isolation:

Stage One: Protest

This is the state of self-pity. The individual feels sad and angry and protests his or her lack of relationships. Poutiness, moodiness, and cantankerousness are common. At this state, the disappointments remain more outward than inward. Common behaviors during this stage include putting up defense mechanisms, such as overworking or concentrating on nothing but business to avoid dealing with the circumstances. During this stage, one begins to deny the need for other people and the desire for relationships.

Stage Two: Depression

At this point, the individual begins to lose hope that his or her needs will ever be met and depression sets in. Also, the anger and negative meditation on disappointments in past relationships become more inward than outward. Common behaviors during this stage are devaluation and projection. Devaluation occurs when the individual begins to devalue or lessen the importance of love and relationships. Projection occurs during this stage when a person projects or extends their personal issues, fears, or values incorrectly onto other people.

Stage Three: Detachment

Now the individual is out of touch with both his or her own needs and the needs of others. The individual now operates in a perpetual state of denial, pretending not to need the affirmation and fellowship of others. They fully deny their foundational need for relationships and, ultimately, alter their personality and limit their development and growth.

In its extreme state, this stage can lead to psychotic and deranged behavior. At this stage, the common behavior is called "reaction formation," which means that now the individual does the opposite of what they really want to do. Total denial occurs and is often accompanied by a spirit of self-hatred. Self-hatred develops through both real and perceived rejection.

Now that we have looked at the stages of isolation, you are in a better position to do a self-examination.

How are your relationships? Every woman of God needs at least one friend or mentor to whom she can vent and with whom she can laugh, receive instruction, or just let down her guard.

If you do not have any friends, you need to ask yourself, "Have I shown myself friendly?" (See Proverbs 18:24.) Some translate this scripture as: "If you want friends, be a friend." Do you often talk yourself out of forming relationships? Are you easily offended or lack trust when it comes to forming bonds with people? You may not believe this is spiritual, but your ability to relate to people is very spiritual. As a matter of fact, God has a problem with people who pretend to be so spiritual and close to Him, yet cannot even get along with other people. First John 4:20 puts it this way: "If a man say, I love God and hateth his brother, he is a liar: for he that loveth not his brother whom he hath seen, how can he love a God whom he hath not seen?"

No matter what you have been through, you have to trust somebody. You will miss out on some of the most fulfilling and profitable relationships if you shut off yourself, your family, or ministry from godly, productive relationships because of fear, distrust, and suspicions.

I am by no means saying that you should reveal intimate details to a lot of people. There are some things you only share with your spouse. However, I am saying that you need healthy, godly intimacy with people of like minds and hearts. If you have been hurt and wounded, I want to encourage you to move beyond the betrayal, disloyalty, and hurt to find that sister (or brother) that has been raised up to bring healing, encouragement, and help to your life.

Please remember that if you are struggling in this area, you have a root of unforgiveness that must be broken. There is nothing that has happened to you that you are not required to forgive. I know that it's tight—but it's right!

I, personally, know the power of relationships and how God will use them to restore your soul. I have been wounded in relationships through betrayal, disloyalty, slander, lies, abuse, etc....so I understand how hard it is to trust anybody when you go through a season where it looks like you have been hurt by everybody! However, I am a witness that God will "restore to you the years that the locust hath eaten" (Joel 2:25). If a mate has wounded you, God can restore that. If church people have wounded you, God will heal your wounds. Maybe you were abused as a child by an authority figure; God will bring you spiritual authority figures that will correctly teach you submission through love.

I have noticed that when God restores you, He usually gives you back more than what you thought you lost. God replaced all of the relationships that wounded me with people who far exceeded the standards, talents, abilities, and commitment levels of the people over whom I had previously grieved. Trust God today to lead you to right relationships.

REMAINING A LADY

It is very important for all of the leading ladies to remember the responsibility that comes along with leadership. Strong, powerful, and anointed women of God can still be ladies, still lead, take care of business, pastor churches, walk in apostolic authority or whatever God has ordained you to do, and remain a lady.

There are many women today that do not seem to realize that even though they are in a leadership role, they still need to exercise a level of wisdom if they want men and women to follow them. Yes, I know that it can be difficult for strong women, because some men do not want to be led by women. Nonetheless, with your power of persuasion and the spirit of wisdom in operation, you will be able to accomplish all that has been assigned to you, without being difficult, moody, cantankerous, or generally not spoken of in a positive manner because of your attitude.

Women in particular must have the Spirit of God as they take on the roles in the kingdom that God has for them. I personally know that God is using women in this season in a very special way, but I also know that they are going to need to know how to remain "ladies" just as much as they know how to preach, prophesy, cast out devils, and lead a nation. Remember, you have the power of persuasion like no other. If you develop the patience, power, and perseverance that it takes to persuade, you will save nations like Esther did, win wars like Jael, and proclaim victories like Deborah!

REMINDER

In ministry, you wise-up or crack-up!

CHAPTER 11

HONORING A FOOL TO BE BLESSED BY A KING

*O*NE OF MY favorite stories—one that I like to share with leading ladies—is found in 1 Samuel 25. This story provides insight into God's heart and demonstrates how He is nigh unto them with a broken heart. It tells a wonderful story of gratitude and submission and the reward that will come when we continue to remain blameless before God, trusting Him with all of our hearts—even with the difficult people that may be in our lives.

In a time when David was traveling throughout the land, trying to avoid being killed by King Saul, he sent some of his men to Nabal, a man of Maon who was shearing sheep in Carmel. (See 1 Sam. 25:5–12.) Nabal rudely refused David's appeal to feed his 600 men, even though Nabal was more than able to accommodate David's request. The custom of the day was that travelers were to be fed, no matter how many there were. David was not asking for a handout. David and his men had protected Nabal's flock while in the area, so the request for food was based on an expected courtesy. Nabal's blatant disrespect for David, his men, and the benefit they had provided through their protection incensed David. He set out to kill Nabal and his household. However, Nabal, the fool (v. 25, NIV), had one asset of which he was not aware, and that was his wife, Abigail.

When Abigail heard how Nabal insulted David, she quickly went into action without telling her husband. She lost no time gathering as much food as she could, jumped on her donkey, and met up with David. She asked for forgiveness regarding her husband's actions and David accepted her apology and her gifts. David's blessing to Abigail is noteworthy. He said:

> "Praise be to the Lord, the God of Israel, who has sent you today to meet me. May you be blessed for your good judgment and for keeping me from bloodshed this day and from avenging myself with my own hands. Otherwise, as surely as the Lord, the God of Israel, lives, who has kept me from harming you, if you had not come quickly to meet me, not one male belonging to Nabal would have been left alive by daybreak." Then David accepted from her hand what she had brought him and said, "Go home in peace. I have heard your words and granted your request."
>
> —1 Samuel 25:32–35, NIV

If Abigail had not intervened, if she had instead taken a passive stance in this potentially deadly situation, there would have been much bloodshed. There continues to be many modern-day Abigail's that need to grab hold of the wisdom, courage, and sometimes quick decisions that are necessary for survival when you are involved with a fool or someone making a foolish decision. This holds true whether it involves the ministry, children, finances, or anything that is potentially devastating. Abigail had an assurance, confidence, and ability to respond quickly to a situation that would have greatly affected her entire household. How often have women, the builders of the house, sat by painstakingly bewildered, wondering whether God was going to intervene when what they really needed to do was get up and use their good judgment, intercession, and action to prevent a foreseeable disaster?

Many women lack what Abigail utilized to save her house: the power of persuasion. This is a woman's greatest weapon. Eve persuaded Adam to eat of the fruit, Delilah persuaded Sampson to tell her the secret of his strength, and Mary persuaded Jesus to perform His first miracle after He told her it was not yet time!

Proverbs 14:1 tell us, "Every wise woman buildeth her house," and she does so with wisdom and understanding. Sometimes having wisdom and understanding means that as you are led by the Spirit of God (and you better make sure that you are), you may sometimes have to do something with which your spouse or others may not be in agreement. I know that religious people may want to tell you to just pray or that God will work it out. I am here to tell you that

I have seen some Abigail's (not Jezebel's) led by the Spirit of God who have prevented their marriages, ministries, money, and minds from total disaster and devastation because of their confidence in knowing the voice of God. Just like biblical Abigail, their confidence gave them a great recompense of reward.

After Abigail saved her house, she returned to a drunken Nabal who was throwing a party. She waited until he was sober in the morning to tell him what she had done. The Bible says that Nabal's "heart died within him, and he became as a stone" (1 Sam. 25:37). As soon as David heard that this fine woman of wisdom was available, he sent for Abigail to be his wife. The Bible says that she quickly jumped on her donkey to once again become the wife of a ruler. (Abigail was also wise enough not to hesitate when she saw a blessing.)

So, what does this story reveal to us? It teaches that God rewarded Abigail for her faithfulness and *her* respect and honor for authority. Many times, women mistakenly go along with foolish and sometimes disrespectful decisions under the guise of being "submitted."

For a woman to disobey a foolish request from a person in authority, she must, first of all, be Spirit-led and have a confident relationship with God. Secondly, the cause for this type of action should be something that is a serious hazard to her family, ministry, etc, and not just a simple or non-threatening incident. Since she is led by the Spirit of God, she should never need worry about going wrong, because He is her final authority and her ultimate submission is to Him.

Abigail was in a situation, as you may be also, over

which she really had no control. And one would wonder how such a noteworthy woman would be with such a fool? (Tell me you haven't seen this before?) Well, undoubtedly Nabal acquired Abigail through an arranged marriage and a handsome dowry, which was the acceptable custom of that day. Because Nabal was rich, he could afford the beautiful and intelligent Abigail as his wife.

In observing this story closely, we can see that Abigail's remarkable submission to the Father's authority and her husband's authority was unwavering. Abigail had a prime opportunity to give her husband over to David, which would have caused Nabal's annihilation and released Abigail from her marriage vows. But she chose to act like a virtuous woman rather than a vengeful wife.

I pray that all the Abigails will be encouraged, strengthened, and fully persuaded that as you continue to obey God, He will also bring peace to your situation. Remember, God does not hold you accountable for what happens *to* you, but He does hold you accountable for what happens *in* you. Since the Bible described Nabal as "churlish and evil in his doings" (1 Sam. 25:3), which translates to foolish, as well as being mean, Abigail had probably been mistreated and abused. She had a very difficult person on her hands. However, in God's faithfulness, He delivered her in due season. Because she honored a fool, she was blessed by a king!

Ladies, do not allow difficult people or situations to disqualify you from your reigning season. Bear in mind, God "will restore to you the years that the locust hath eaten" (Joel 2:25). As you continue to remain blameless before God, you can be confident that "the glory of this latter house shall be greater than of the former" (Hag. 2:9). God has to honor His word—so whatever way He plans to improve your situation, know that "better is the end of a thing than the beginning thereof" (Eccles. 7:8). Rise up Abigail and take your stand, because it is not what you're going through that is important, but it is what you're coming to!

CHAPTER 12

WALKING IN YOUR DESTINY

*N*OW THAT I have spoken to you as a father and overseer (both of whom I am), my prayer is that you would be like the Bereans, who received the word of Paul the Apostle "with all readiness of mind, and searched the scriptures daily, whether those things were so" (Acts 17:11). Study the Scriptures pertaining to godly living as saints of God and, more specifically, as godly women. Allow the Holy Spirit to minister the truth of His Word and bring conviction for change.

God has placed gifts and talents in you and planned a destiny for you before the foundations of the world. My desire for you is that you walk out your manifested destiny as the powerfully anointed woman of God that He has made you, and that your life will be like that of the virtuous woman of God in Proverbs 31, where your children (naturally and/or spiritually) will rise up and call you blessed; and your husband not only will call you blessed, but he will continue to praise you (Proverb 31:28).

Finally, God gave us examples of godly women in His Word, so that the leading ladies in ministry who come after them would learn from them. So, take your place among the Ruths, the Esthers, and the other virtuous First Ladies and women of God and watch God use you to turn the world upside down!

WHAT EVERY LEADING LADY NEEDS TO KNOW

How to Recognize the Fragmented Soul

As a woman of God, called to lead and deliver His people, there are some basic things you must know to be an effective leader, to walk in discernment, and to provide sound counsel. Particularly in your ministry to other women, God has given you a responsibility to teach them the very foundation of how to function as ladies, wives, and mothers.

Titus 2:3–5 says:

> The aged women likewise, that they be in behaviour as becometh holiness, not false accusers, not given to much wine, teachers of good things; That they may teach the young women to be sober, to love their husbands, to love their children, To be discreet, chaste, keepers at home, good, obedient to their own husbands, that the word of God be not blasphemed.

We all know that a human being consists of a body, a soul, and a spirit. We often give attention to our physical being and even to our spirit man. Yet, we have sometimes overlooked the state of the soul of the people to which we are called, and this can limit our ability to be effective.

Most of us, when we came to the Lord, were fragmented (scattered) in some way. We have been able to exist and function, yet we are still broken in different areas of our soul—areas of our emotions, feelings, thoughts, imaginations, etc. Scattering is a curse that we come under as a result of sin.

When we sin, pieces of the person God intended for us to be are left behind. We trade our purity, blessings, health, and parts of God's perfect plan for a sin we have committed. Thus, parts of the whole person God purposed for us to be lie scattered along the paths of our lives at each point where we have chosen to sin.

First Thessalonians 5:23 says, "And the very God of peace sanctify you wholly; and I pray God your whole spirit and soul and body be preserved blameless unto the coming of our Lord Jesus Christ." This scripture shows us that God's interest in sanctifying us is not limited to our spiritual being, but to the whole person.

Therefore, in order to be able to teach, we must have a revelation of the fragmented soul so that we will recognize the characteristics and implement effective ministry to those whose souls have been scattered through trauma, trials, circumstances, or sin.

The concept of dealing with a person holistically did not originate in the Far East or in New Age thinking. It originated with God. Many times Jesus' message was one of wholeness, such as when He said in the Gospels, "Thy faith hath made thee whole." Why? It is because sin can leave you scattered.

Sin affects each part of you. (Read Proverbs 6:32 for an

example.) Many people are facing illnesses because of sin in their lives. Every cause does not show on an x-ray or test result. (See the list of ten sicknesses associated with the state of the soul.)

Sometimes as saints, we often are not effective in true ministry to the soul. What do I mean by that? I mean, we have to make sure spiritual problems are resolved in a spiritual way and recognize that soulish problems have to often be dealt with in a special order or sequence. Let me give you an example:

In Luke 6:17–49, Jesus is with a great multitude, and many of them "were vexed with unclean spirits" (v. 18). So, Jesus first healed the people and then He began to teach them how to treat one another. Jesus demonstrated that you do not get very far, no matter how good the teaching is, when the people whom you are teaching are vexed or fragmented. Therefore, they are not truly receiving your ministry if they have not first been delivered. Of course, it is true that the Word delivers, but we have to be able to discern the cases requiring deliverance as a prerequisite to teaching the Word of God. Depending on the state of the individual, teaching ahead of deliverance could be like taking a bath with your clothes on.

Wholeness comes not through treatment, but by healing. When Jesus said, "Your faith hath made you whole," He was saying, "I am the Healer and Restorer and by trusting in Me, you have received your wholeness."

Restoration, therefore, is a holistic process involving spirit, soul, and body. Only God has the power to gather the scattered pieces of our sin-ridden lives and bring them back to wholeness. Not only you, my sister, but every member of the body of Christ must allow the Holy Spirit to do a continual work within us, empowering us to live victorious Christian lives. It is He who does the work of restoring our fragmented lives as we yield to His direction and gain access to all that the Father has for us.

Fragmented people are often characterized by having problems trusting others and having serious anger problems. They usually have an inability to respond and are often poor communicators. Fragmented people have difficulty making decisions, moving on, letting go, or making long-term commitments. Fragmented people have a faulty preceptor and they process everything through their woundedness, hurts, and circumstances.

When God restores souls to wholeness, He allows His personality to shine through our repaired personalities, as all of us are made in God's image and all of our personalities are a reflection of some part of God Himself.

As a leading lady called to deliver God's people, you must recognize that every person, every marriage, and every circumstance may differ. You need to be able to differentiate whether someone's actions are a result of him or her not being saved or a result of their soul being fragmented. We do know that the benefits of healing are available once we are saved, yet if the soul is fragmented, there are special steps that need to be taken in order to get the person to a place of wholeness.

For detailed and specific information on how to minister to the fragmented soul, see the recommended reading section of the appendix.

SICKNESS AND THE SOUL

Let me first state emphatically that this list has been given to me by the Spirit of God, compiled over my 30+ years of experience. It is not scientific, nor does it stand as a diagnosis; neither am I stating that these conditions are always the cause behind the particular sicknesses listed. However, I am saying that in my 30+ years of experience, having prayed for millions of people, having over 25,000 people come through my churches, and the countless encounters, counseling, and deliverance of which I have been a part, I have seen clear and consistent patterns that often exist in the following:

Sickness (Problem)	Soul State
Eye blotches	Woundedness
Heart Attacks	Disobedience/rebellion/anger
Lungs/Internal Organs	Stress
Arthritis	Unforgiveness, unconfessed sin
Vaginal problems	Anger, unforgiveness, bitterness
Breasts/Lumps	Loneliness
Barrenness	Generational Curse

TOP 30 MISTAKES FOR LEADING LADIES TO AVOID

- Outshining Christ (through lasciviousness, carnality, etc.)

- Not having a consistent prayer life

- Not praying for yourself, your spouse, your children, other loved ones, and your vision daily

- Being led by your emotions

- Competing (with your mate or others)

- Comparing yourself, mate, and ministry with others

- Not understanding or supporting the vision of the house

- Not supporting your mate or leadership

- Not developing yourself, remaining immature

- Not discovering or recognizing your mentor

- Lacking courage (If you can't face it, you can't erase it!)

- Staying in the past (a mistake is a chance to begin again intelligently)

- Not attending business meetings and knowing what is going on

- Not taking time for yourself

- Not learning from mistakes (A problem unlearned is a problem returned.)

- Being paralyzed by risk instead of focusing on the reward

- Trying to understand everything (God does not always speak to you when you ask Him, He speaks to you when you can understand.)

- Having excuses for not doing the right thing

- Trying to be friends with the sheep

- Telling the sheep too much of your personal business

- Not coming to church regularly

- Not taking time to receive ministry

- Wearing inappropriate clothing

- Being moody, fussy, arrogant, and untouchable

- Having a rich house, but a sloppy church

- Allowing your children to be out of control

- Coming late to church

- Not keeping your word

- Having out-of-control spending

- Not connecting to the people, particularly the women

APOSTOLIC NUGGETS

**It's not what happened to you,
it's what happened in you!**

Advice is like medicine, it does no good if you don't take it.

**If God doesn't deliver you from something,
it's because you have to go through.**

The first time something happens to you,
you are a victim, the second time you are a volunteer.

You cannot grow using yourself as a role model.

Your past is not your potential; you forfeit your future
by staying in the past.

Don't complain about what you permit.

Your friends never need any explanation
and your enemies will never believe any explanation.

The faith that can't be tested can't be trusted!

It's not what you are eating; it's what's eating you.

The way you see yourself is reflected in your choices.

Your character is reflected in your decisions.

**If Satan can get you focused on your matters,
he knows he has you distracted from God's matters.**

When you discover your destiny, you also encounter your
greatest enemy—your mind!

There are no shortcuts to anywhere worth going.

If you want to change your level of faith,
change your level of obedience.

Sometimes God has to separate to educate.

If you keep doing what you have always done,
you will keep on having what you have always had.

Ten Things Men Want Most in a Woman

1. **Friend** (someone to bond with he can trust)

2. **Admiration** (cheerleader, men gravitate to women who admire them, run from those critical of them)

3. **Empathy** (support)

4. **Sex** (Men are microwaves, women are ovens)

5. **Pretty wife** (men are vision-oriented)

6. **Intercessor** (stand in the gap)

7. **Mother's heart** (knowing how to teach him with love)

8. **Help** (keeping him balanced, filling the gaps of his weakness)

9. **Submission** (subject until the mission is complete)

10. **Homemaker** (Generally not of great concern to most, but more to some)

RECOMMENDED READING

Turner, Clifford E., Ph.D. *Recovery: Understanding and Dealing with Life's Traumas.* New Jersey: The Wine Press, 2000.

Crawford, Beverly "Bam," D.D. *The Power of the Soul: The Authority of Thought Control—Part 1.* Culver City: Bam Crawford Publishing, 2005.